# PREPARATION PRECEDES POWER

*How Successful Missionaries
Prepare to Serve*

*by*

RANDY L. BOTT

**Millennial Press, Inc.**
576 S. Commerce Road, Suite #3
Orem, UT 84058

ISBN: #1-932597-06-9

# CONTENTS

*To our six children who have all responded to the Lord's call to serve. Especially to Landon who is waiting to enter the MTC at the time of this printing. To the hundreds of missionaries who served with us in the California, Fresno Mission. To the thousands of preparing missionaries who have sequenced through my missionary preparation classes at BYU and who asked the difficult questions requiring countless hours of study and prayerful meditation to provide meaningful answers. Finally to my beloved companion, Vickie, who is a living example of what a true missionary really is— I dedicate this volume with a prayer that the principles and doctrines contained herein will motivate members and missionaries to share this glorious gospel with the people in every nation on earth.*

*A special thanks to Deseret Book and cited General Authorities for permission to use their copyrighted materials.*

# INTRODUCTION

The scene is tense. Anticipation is high. A special meeting has been called. You have never seen this many gathered in one stadium at one time — 110,000 people. But this isn't to watch a sports event. Word is that the Savior will appear and select one person to be His traveling companion on a special mission to prepare the world for His Second Coming.

Instead of the loud, boisterous cheers and rowdy, undisciplined behavior commonly seen at large sports gatherings, there is near silence. It couldn't contrast more with anything you have ever witnessed! Then in an instant the Resurrected Savior appears and moves to the podium where He will name the one lucky person who will be honored to go with Him. Noting the sea of humanity in the stadium, you have little hope that you will be selected. Can you sense the shock, the thrill, and the disbelief when the Savior calls your name as His traveling companion?

You may think this is just the imagination of a dreamer. However, it is not. Some elementary mathematics will prove the point. There are approximately 6.6 billion people living on earth at the present time. There are approximately 11 million members of the Church. Simple division reveals that only one in every six hundred people on earth is a Latter-day Saint. However, Satan has cleverly deceived about half of the members of the Church into believing that going to Church on Sunday is not that important. Again doing simple division, you have about a one in twelve hundred chance of being an active Latter-day Saint today. However, the odds really get pumped up when you consider that there are just over 60,000 full-time missionaries. Sixty thousand divided into 6.6 billion equals one in 110,000!

Wearing the "black name tag" is an honor that very few will ever have in mortality. You were saved for this very hour! It is not by chance that you are alive now, living in the your present condition, and preparing for a full-time mission. President Ezra Taft Benson spoke about you, outlining his prophetic vision of who you are and what lies ahead of you:

For nearly six thousand years, God has held you in reserve to make your appearance in the final days before the Second Coming of the Lord[...] While our generation will be comparable in wickedness to the days of Noah, when the Lord cleansed the earth by flood, there is a major difference this time. It is that God has saved for the final inning some of his strongest children, who will help bear off the Kingdom triumphantly. And that is where you come in, for you are the generation that must be prepared to meet your God.

All through the ages the prophets have looked down through the corridors of time to our day. Billions of the deceased and those yet to be born have their eyes on us. Make no mistake about it — you are a marked generation. There has never been more expected of the faithful in such a short period of time as there is of us. Never before on the face of this earth have the forces of evil and the forces of good been as well organized. Now is the great day of the devil's power, with the greatest mass murders of all time living among us. But now is also the great day of the Lord's power, with the greatest number ever of priesthood holders on the earth. And the showdown is fast approaching ("In His Steps," in *Speeches of the Year,* 1979 Provo: BYU Press, 1980, page 59).

Think of it: saved for 6000 years and given the special privilege of preparing the world for the Savior's Second Coming! Later in the book, when we discuss the Plan of Salvation, you will see how you came to be so special. Right now it would be well to seriously think about what President Benson said. All the way through this book you will be asked to see if you need an attitude adjustment or some behavior modification to live up to who you really are and make the necessary preparations to fulfill what you were foreordained to become.

Sometimes when our leaders talk about being "the chosen youth" we are inclined to think we are somewhat better than anyone else. Elder Dean L. Larsen forcefully taught:

> Tonight I would like to talk principally to the young men of the Aaronic Priesthood about the responsibility you have to live in such a way that you can be a good influence in your home, whatever the conditions there may be, and so that you can qualify to do all the Lord expects of you during your lifetime.
>
> Young men, I do not believe that you are here upon the earth at this time by accident. I believe you qualified in the premortal life to come into mortality at a time when great things would be required of you. I believe you demonstrated before you came here that you were capable of being trusted under unusually difficult circumstances — that you could measure up to the most difficult challenges. Don't misunderstand me. I don't suggest that you are

inherently better than or superior to any of the other generations that have come to the earth. You do not automatically qualify for any more blessings or advantages than anyone else who has lived since the earth was created. You can go astray, become involved in transgression, and incur the judgments of God as readily as any who have preceded you here. In fact, you live in an environment in which it is probably as easy to disqualify yourselves in this way as any generation has ever experienced. But God trusts that you will not. He relies upon you to keep yourselves eligible to accomplish the monumental tasks that he expects you to achieve. (Conference Report, April 1983)

All you have to do to know that Elder Larsen and President Benson saw our day is to watch television, view almost any DVD, listen to the music the world promotes as "good," read the newspaper about what the youth of the world are doing regarding drugs, sex, violence, lack of direction, etc., and you will know that the world is ripening for destruction. It isn't easy to stay clean in such a filthy world, but God expects that you will. Elder Neal A. Maxwell said:

My beloved friends, you are the vanguard of the righteous spirits to be infused into the Church in the last days. Back beyond time, it was so determined, and you were prepared — before the foundations of the world — to help save others in the latter-day world.

You cannot keep that resplendent rendezvous if you become like the world! Make your righteous marks on the world instead of being spotted by the world.

Be true, now, to your emotions of long ago when, as the Lord set in motion His plan of Salvation and laid the foundation of this earth, "The morning stars sang together, and all the sons (and daughters) of God shouted for joy" (Job 38:7). (Young Adult Fireside on Temple Square, 23 June 1985)

Every church leader who has spoken directly to the youth of the church has said the same thing: "You are special. You were reserved to come at this time. There is much expected of you. You can't look, act, talk, recreate, do drugs, or be like the youth of the world and still fulfill the foreordination you had earned the right to have before the foundations of the world were ever laid."

As we now talk about how to be a more effective missionary, take time frequently to do a mid-course correction, if necessary, so that when the hour of your mission comes you will be right on target to be among the greatest generation of missionaries ever to be born on this earth. Don't be discouraged if you have some growing and changing to do before you can be a modern day Ammon. If the Lord didn't know you could succeed, He wouldn't have put you down here at this time. You may have some serious questions as to whether you can succeed — God, who knows the end from the beginning, does not!

I will now write to who you can become, not necessarily to who you are at this time. If you will read by the power of the Spirit and if I can write by the power of the Spirit, we will understand one another and you'll get the spiritual motivation necessary to prepare now for the greatest experiences of your life (to this point) — a full time mission.

*Chapter 1*

# CALLED TO SERVE AND NOT TO BE SERVED

All of us are thrilled as we sing the hymn "Called to Serve." As explained in the introductory chapter, it is no small privilege to be numbered among those on the Lord's first team in the final minutes of the fourth quarter of the Super Bowl of all time. As you would expect, and as we will enlarge upon later, Satan will do everything in his power to slow the work and divert the focus of the workers — the missionaries.

One of the tactics the devil uses most effectively is the subtle shift in expectations of the mission field. He whispers that because you are "the chosen generation" you somehow should merit preferential treatment. Perhaps you shouldn't have to work as hard as those who are not "the chosen generation." In fact, given your elite status, you should actually be the ones who are served. But if you are going to become like the Savior, whom you represent, you must do as He did. "Even as the Son of man came not to be ministered unto, but to minister, and to give his life a ransom for many" (Matthew 20:28). Learning how to "give your life" for your investigators, members, and missionary companions gives you invaluable experience that will benefit you for the rest of mortality as a married person, and for your endless eternal life.

If your pre-mission life has unfolded as Divinely planned, you have transitioned from having everything done for you as an infant, to becoming increasingly independent as a youth, and on to not only caring for yourself but actually shouldering some responsibility to assist in the work as a young adult. Unfortunately, without the benefit of demanding farm labor, large gardens, cows to milk, herds to feed, and sprinkler pipe to move, too many young people have grown up without making these essential transitions.

Mowing the lawn often takes only a few minutes. Taking out the garbage is a three-times-a-week task. Cleaning your room may only happen on Saturday morning. Now you enter the mission field and you are expected to study, prepare, proselyte, and serve others for sixteen hours a day — every day! Too many missionaries have not connected the dots — mission work really is work! One of the major challenges faced by mission leaders is motivating missionaries to work hard the entire day, come home dog tired, and do it again day after endless day.

How can you best prepare? By disciplining yourself to stick with each assigned task until it is finished, no matter how distasteful the task. You can increase your drive by getting a part-time job that requires sacrifice of sleeptime and/or playtime. Not only will it add to your mission fund, but it will get you in the habit of being on task, on time, being responsible for fulfilling your commitment. Take some additional responsibility around the house. Volunteer to do the dishes, clean up the kitchen after meals, help with the wash, vacuum the house, organize the garage, tackle the storage shed, weed the flower beds, edge the lawn — the list goes on.

As you identify some of the things you will be expected to do as a missionary, you can easily see the benefits of the pre-game warm-up. You will be expected to cook a majority of your own meals. Work with your mom or older sister or dad or whoever does the cooking. Learn how to cook your favorite meals, prepare fast but nutritious meals, learn how to make a shopping list so that the foods you buy are those necessary to make your favorite dishes. Go shopping often with the shopper in your home. Ask questions like you used to when you were really young. "Why buy this brand over that one?" "Why buy the larger size rather than the smaller size?" "How do you recognize when a 'good buy' is really a good buy and not just the store's attempt to unload outdated or inferior products?" "Why do we shop after we eat rather than before?" The list of questions is only limited by your ability to think and foresee some of the problems you'll face and then seek to find the answers. Nothing is difficult if you know how to do it. Don't assume that managing the essential parts of home life is so easy that you don't need teaching.

Learn how to do the laundry. As a mission president it was disconcerting to see how many missionaries came to our mission with crisp, white shirts, and then to see them at the first round of zone conferences with murky gray shirts. Washing darks and whites together doesn't work. Equally as disappointing were the number of missionaries who came with dark pants or skirts with bleached spots on them. Bleach and darks don't do well together.

When you are either too smart to be taught or not concerned enough to pay the price to learn, the lessons will still be learned, but the expense and embarrassment will be considerably higher in the mission field. You can save yourself a lot of grief if you will immerse yourself in that phase of your education prior to your mission.

Personal hygiene is an area often missed but essential to

effective missionary work. I received a phone call one day from a sister who complained that her companion only showered once a week and never used deodorant. In our mission the temperatures often soared above 100 degrees on a daily basis during the summer months. Even some of the faithful members were requesting that the sisters not come to visit until the offending sister was transferred.

I asked the sister who had called why she didn't handle the problem and she informed me that her companion refused to listen to her, accusing her of just trying to "put me down." I asked her to put her companion on the phone. Over the protests of the offending sister, I asked why a sister of her spiritual stature would be content to serve without the Spirit. She responded by saying that she enjoyed the Spirit on a daily basis. To which I responded that she couldn't enjoy the Spirit when she disobeyed the mission rules. She said she prided herself in keeping all the mission rules. Then I referred her to the white handbook (i.e. "White Bible") used as a guidebook for all missionaries, and had her read the part that states: "Be neat and clean. Bathe frequently and use deodorant..." (Page 15). I explained that a missionary cannot enjoy the Spirit if they are disobedient. She thanked me (although I don't think her "thanks" was sincere) and hung up. A week later the sister who called complaining about her companion called again. She asked: "What did you say to my companion?" I asked why she was questioning. She said: "Ever since your talk with her she has been showering every morning, at lunch, and at night and uses deodorant between every house we visit!"

Once this diligent sister discovered that personal hygiene was essential to effective missionary work, and because she desired more than anything to be an effective missionary, she was willing to learn a lesson she should have learned years before entering the mission field. Ask your parents or leaders if you need to increase the attention you give to your personal hygiene.

You have been born into and raised in a "what's in it for me?" world. It is a rare young man or woman who has resisted the devil-inspired enticement to be self-centered. The more "outward focused" you can become before your mission, the easier the transition will be when you hit the mission field. You have been placed in an environment (home!) where there are endless opportunities to serve. Especially if you are the oldest child (or near the top), you may have been tempted to use your age, size, and strength to get what you want. Many family battles have been started by older children using their privileged position to bully little brothers or sisters. If you have fallen into the habit, you will be light-years ahead if you can eliminate that trait from your character. You won't be the biggest, the oldest, the strongest missionary in the field. Even if you are and try to use your size or strength to bully others, you'll find that your mission will end much sooner than your prophet-generated call. What a shame to be sent home because you haven't learned to get along and resolve differences without resorting to force. If you need some changes, do yourself a favor and start working on them now!

Another major shock for so many missionaries is failed expectations. They expect people in the mission field to feed them a meal a day. Are the people supposed to help feed the missionaries? Yes! What if the missionaries expect it and for some reason the people don't come through? Often the missionaries become angry and say or do things which puts a distance between themselves and the members. Without the help and support of the members, the missionary work is slowed to a near-stop. It would be far better to learn to expect nothing and then express sincere gratitude whenever anything is done for you.

Being willing to recognize and express appreciation for the least kindness you receive is called by President Thomas S. Monson "the attitude of gratitude"(*Church News*, April 11, 1992, p.17). In our mission we found that people responded much better to expressions of gratitude than they did from public or private chastisement for what they failed to do.

The best place to learn "the attitude of gratitude" is in your home. How long has it been since you sincerely expressed appreciation to mom for washing your clothes, preparing your meals, cleaning up after you, being there when you come home from your dates, giving counsel when you've been hurt or shunned, or a thousand other little things that moms do? When was the last time you thanked dad for providing a home for you to live in, transportation to and from activities, clothes you wear, food you eat, words of encouragement when you are having a tough time, and a thousand other things dad does all the time but you often take for granted? Perhaps there is a leader, a teacher, a friend, a neighbor, a relative who has done something for you and you just didn't think to thank. In your prayers how often do you thank Heavenly Father for sacrificing His Son for you, for creating the earth for you to live on, for providing daily counsel through living prophets, for the wisdom of the ages as recorded in the scriptures, for the constant guidance of His Holy Spirit?

When you develop the "attitude of gratitude" and determine that you are born to serve and not to be served, your life takes on a whole new dimension. One of the important and immediate benefits is that you take away others power to "make you mad, sad, or bad." You see, if you expect nothing and no one does anything for you, it is okay. If you expect someone to do something for you, and they are supposed to do it but don't, then you become agitated and begin to lose faith in family members, friends, leaders, and others who are supposed to be serving you but are not.

Try it and see if it works for you. Expect nothing, express gratitude for everything, and move ahead without feelings of bitterness when someone fails to come through. As you become increasingly aware of how much is done for you and consistently express appreciation for what is done, you'll discover that many more things are being done than you had ever imagined. People are much more inclined to sacrifice for you if they feel their sacrifice is appreciated. The Lord even mentions ingratitude as one of two things that anger him. "And in nothing doth man offend God, or against none is his wrath kindled, save those who confess not his hand in all things, and obey not his commandments" (D&C 59:21). You may remember the story of the ten lepers who were cured by the Savior of that dreaded disease (see Luke 17:10-19). As you re-read the account you can feel the disappointment in the Savior's question "Were there not ten cleansed? but where are the nine?"

Don't be numbered among the nine ungrateful lepers. Start now by being attentive to everything that is done for you by family, friends, leaders, and especially by the Lord. Then make up your mind that you will enter the service of the Master determined to work hard all day every day without expecting praise or recognition. As you develop these godly qualities, you will find that God sends His Spirit to you in ever-increasing amounts. That Spirit will "enlighten your mind, which shall fill your soul with joy" (D&C 11:13). It is the presence of the Spirit which enables missionaries to face constant rejection, persecution, and taunting and still walk away with joy in their hearts. If you expect your reinforcement or praise to come horizontally (i.e. from what other people do or say for you) you will be setting yourself up for disappointment. If you are willing to take your praise from the Vertical (i.e. from God), then you become virtually immune from the depressive attacks by Satan and his followers.

## Chapter 2

# IF YE ARE PREPARED YE SHALL NOT FEAR

Many young people, as they anticipate a mission, have an overwhelming sense of inadequacy. That is normal and is not bad. If you are too confident in your own abilities, then you are less apt to rely upon the Lord for the help you'll need to be successful. It is somewhat amusing to listen to the Lord define a nineteen year old boy or a twenty-one year old girl. He said: "Wherefore, I call upon the weak things of the world, those who are unlearned and despised" (D&C 35:13). Why would He choose those to represent Him who He knows are so unimpressive? He gives the answer: "to thrash the nations by the power of my Spirit; And their arm shall be my arm, and I will be their shield and their buckler; and I will gird up their loins, and they shall fight manfully for me; and their enemies shall be under their feet; and I will let fall the sword in their behalf, and by the fire of mine indignation will I preserve them' (verses 13-14).

What a marvelous promise! The Savior doesn't want you to try to convert people to yourselves because of your charisma, personality, or intellect. He wants them to "come unto Him" so they can receive eternal life. You are not going to be alone. The Lord promised "for I will go before your face. I will be on your right hand and on your left, and my Spirit shall be in your hearts, and mine angels round about you, to bear you up" (D&C 84:88).

As a new mission president, I was frustrated with one Elder who said: "President, I don't need to memorize the discussions. I have such a strong presence about me that when I teach, the Spirit will convert them. So I am wasting my time studying!" It took some convincing to get the young man to realize that the Lord would convert by the Spirit only after truths had been taught by the missionary. The Lord commanded: "Neither take ye thought beforehand what ye shall say; but treasure up in your minds continually the words of life, and it shall be given you in the very hour that portion that shall be meted unto every man" (D&C 84:85). The "treasuring up in your mind continually" suggests the need to be diligent before, during and after the full time mission. In fact, the Lord outlines a broad array of subjects to round out your learning experience in Doctrine and Covenants 88:78-80, specifically "that ye may be prepared in all things when I shall send you again to magnify the calling whereunto I have called you, and the mission with which I have commissioned you" (D&C 88:80). Just a partial listing includes: doctrines of the gospel, principles of perfection, astronomy, geology, oceanography, history, current events, prophecies, foreign affairs, domestic affairs, wars, geography, etc. Re-read Doctrine and Covenants 88:78-80 to see those and other topics which are included.

In order to have the time to become acquainted with all these areas of learning, we are going to have to be more vigilant, devoting more time to study and less to television, DVDs, movies, games, and recreation. It seems that Satan's tactic in this area is to get young people so caught up in recreation and "fun" that they never find time to prepare adequately for the sacred mission they were foreordained to fulfill. What a tragedy to realize too late that precious years had been wasted, preparation was inadequate, and good people were turned away from embracing the gospel because you wasted your time in fun but non-productive recreational activities.

Since preparation precedes presentation, we could all stand to be more serious about preparing. How can we do this? The obvious answer is to read the scriptures daily. If a person studied one hour a day from age twelve to nineteen, over 2550 hours would have been spent in "feasting upon the words of Christ" (see 2 Nephi 32:3). Add to that the 364 hours spent in Sunday School classes, the same number of hours in Priesthood or Young Women's classes, and the 720 hours spent in Seminary, you can see that there are multiple opportunities to "learn of me" (D&C 19:23) and become familiar with His word. However, too often young people either absent themselves from those classes or pay less than stellar attention to what is being discussed.

If I had it to do all over again, I would be actively participating in every class, every fireside, every bishop's youth fireside, etc., that I could. It would have saved me from the following embarrassing experience (which is not unique to me!): The very day I arrived in Samoa to begin my first mission, the district leader who met us at the plane took us new "greenies" to visit a Catholic priest who had been in Samoa for fourteen years. He was a kindly man but over the years had watched people leave his congregation to join the Lord's true church. He had studied our doctrine to find out what was so appealing. As a result of his study, he knew our doctrine far better than I did.

After the casual, congenial "getting to know you" conversation, he systematically took our doctrine and beat me about the head and shoulders. He asked questions I had never thought of. He pointed out what he considered to be contradictions between what "Mormons believe and what the Bible teaches," he ridiculed living prophets and personal revelation. By the time he finished, if there had been a plane back to Hawaii, I would have been on it. Fortunately for me, the plane only came once a week. By the next week I was settled on the back of a distant island and not able to get to the airport.

I didn't quickly forget the feelings of anger, regret, disappointment, and frustration I felt as this kindly priest revealed my total ignorance. I vowed there and then never to be so unprepared that anyone from another religion could attack the Lord's true religion in my presence without meeting overwhelming resistence by reason, by logic, by the scriptures, and by the Spirit. To complete the story: six months later I was being transferred to an area that required I pass through that same village where the priest lived. In the fourteen years he had been there, he had only mastered the very basic greetings in Samoan. Blessed with the gift of tongues, I had become relatively fluent in Samoan in those six months. Because of my resolve never to be embarrassed again, I had studied every free minute so I could document our beliefs from the Bible and explain them in greater clarity using the modern scriptures. I visited the priest and returned the favor — I beat him about the head and shoulders with our doctrine using his scriptures, and (hopefully) punctuated by the witness of the Spirit. I probably shouldn't have been so aggressive but as I freely conversed with his Samoan helpers in their native tongue, they seemed genuinely impressed that I had mastered a language and a gospel in six short months.

However, the regrettable part is that I was so woefully unprepared the day I started my mission. It has been a lifelong goal to help others avoid the embarrassingly painful experience of knowing the gospel is true and yet being unable to defend it.

I have been teaching young men and young women who were preparing for missions for over thirty years. In that time I've interfaced with literally thousands of pre-missionaries. Although you are definitely better prepared and more spiritually sensitive than I was as a young man, there is still much to be done before you are fully prepared to serve. So in addition to reading the scriptures and attending church meetings and Seminary, consider the following list of activities which will give you experience so you won't be unprepared when your mission call arrives.

Missionaries talk a lot. Learn to talk informally with adults, young adults, old people, children, or anyone who will listen to you. Learn to express yourself, your ideas, your questions, your thoughts in a way that is clear, articulate, and non-offensive. Too often the language the kids use is totally unacceptable to those who are educated or older. Since you are there to serve them, it is you that must adjust your vocabulary. It is true that the people of the world should be more tolerant and understanding, but that isn't likely to happen.

If you would like an exercise in understanding your responsibility to act, dress, talk, behave, and eat in a way that does not offend people, read Romans 14 and substitute dress, or speech, or attitudes or what you eat or drink for the words "meat and drink." You may be surprised that Paul puts the burden not to offend squarely on the messenger — not those hearing the message. For example consider verses 13 and 15: "Let us not therefore judge one another any more: but judge this rather, that no man put a stumblingblock or an occasion to fall in his brother's way [...] But if thy brother be grieved with thy meat, now walkest thou not charitably. Destroy not him with thy meat, for whom Christ died." If you substitute "your way of speaking" for "thy meat", you will see that Paul understood that preaching the gospel is far more important than exercising your liberty to dress how you want, talk any way you want, act however you want, or anything else.

If you are willing to ask, I would suspect your parents and other adults would gladly offer suggestions of things you might eliminate or modify so that your speech becomes less offensive. Perhaps you have "arrived" in that area and have nothing to worry about. Does that mean you are prepared? Hardly!

Over the years I have listened to young people (and many old ones, too!) give talks in church meetings. Some do an excellent job, others leave a lot of room for improvement. Why not focus on what you like and dislike in the delivery as well as the content in every meeting you attend? See if you can identify what makes the difference between "an okay talk" and "an outstanding talk." Practice every time you get a chance preparing and delivering talks. Giving inspiring talks is not just standing up and saying whatever comes to your mind. Remember: "If ye are prepared" the Lord will bring to mind in the very moment (see D&C 100:5-8) exactly what He would like taught. But if you are not prepared, then the Lord can not draw water from a dry well.

In my mind's eye I see two missionaries sitting before a family, teaching them eternal truths. What could be closer to duplicating what you will be doing as a missionary than teaching a Family Home Evening lesson or doing your home teaching or visiting teaching? If you take the "easy out" and just read the message from the First Presidency, you will have missed a golden opportunity to learn how to take what is being taught by the living prophets, put the concepts in your own words, use an occasional direct quote, and make it all flow into a logical, understandable, motivational lesson.

With the introduction of the new method of teaching relying more on what the Spirit directs than upon memorized dialogue, young missionaries are being entrusted to recognize the doctrine well enough and the Spirit's promptings clearly enough to fashion their own discussions — or at least to teach the approved principles in the order dictated by the Spirit. Although, as a professional teacher, I don't want someone telling me exactly how to teach, when I was a young, inexperienced missionary, the prospects of teaching by the Spirit without a completely outlined text was somewhat intimidating. It would be like playing at a piano recital — if you have practiced the piece you are to play a thousand times, then playing it in front of a large audience isn't nearly so frightening. If the first time you had ever tried to play the piece was in front of an audience, it is easy to see why gripping fear can cause you to stumble. Prepare now and avoid the embarrassment of stumbling later on.

The present condition of the world (without prospects of great improvement) suggests that you will meet some physical confrontation on your mission. People who don't understand who you are and what you are doing, possibly having been given false information by their church leaders or others, may think they are doing God a favor by persecuting you.

As a young missionary in Samoa we were ordered to cease proselyting by an irate minister from another church. He added the threat that he would have the young adults of his congregation stone us if we didn't leave immediately. Having more courage than good sense, I turned to my companion and suggested that we continue visiting. As we walked down the road adjacent to the beach, rocks about the size of a doubled up fist came flying from the bushes lining the road. We walked about 100 yards without being hit once. I don't know if the young men of the village were just trying to scare us or whether we really were protected by the Lord, but these young men, who could throw a rock forty feet in the air and dislodge a coconut from a palm tree with deadly accuracy, could never hit us.

If I had always "met fire with fire" as a youth, I would have picked up the rocks that fell around us and threw them back. That would have been a fatal mistake. If your adopted method of dealing with confrontation would lead you into a fight, you need to change. Remember the Lord's promise in Doctrine and Covenants 35:13-14 that He would be your shield and your buckler and that He would protect you. That requires a lot of faith on your part, but is also the key to your physical as well as spiritual survival.

For you young men who are preparing to serve, learning to use your priesthood effectively can save a lot of embarrassment and concern. The priesthood is the power of God which He has given you the privilege of using. However, it can only be used to promote the accomplishment of "His will" — not your own personal desires.

Learning to know and understand what the impressions of the Spirit mean isn't something you will master overnight. I remember being dragged from our *fale* (home) at three o'clock in the morning in the middle of a driving rain storm to bless a young man who had eaten something poisonous out of the ocean and was on the brink of death. When I arrived, a frantic father was holding his convulsing son who was frothing at the mouth and whose eyes were rolled back to where only the white parts were visible. The father pleadingly said, "I'm an elder, I have anointed my son. You give him a blessing and heal him!" Although I had serious misgivings about what I should say, I was influenced by the terrified looks of the boy's parents. I laid my hands on his head and commanded him to live. He died with my hands still on his head.

Three weeks later a very similar situation occurred. A young family had eaten something poisonous out of the sea and were deathly ill. Again my companion and I were summoned to give blessings. By the time we arrived the young mother had died. The father was in worse shape than the young boy had been three weeks earlier. I determined that I would just wish him a happy trip into the Spirit World. However, as I laid my hands on his head, I felt the strongest impression to tell him that he would live to raise his children. I wrestled with myself, knowing that if I commanded him to live and he died, I would not only be embarrassed but would have no confidence in my ability to understand the prompting of the Spirit. Reluctantly I commanded the man to live. He opened his eyes and said: "Elder, I don't feel very good. Would you take me to the hospital?"

It has taken many years to learn that the priesthood cannot be used to do something contrary to the will of God. Neither can faith alter the will of God. Both priesthood and faith are to be exercised to understand the will of God so that every blessing given under that Spirit, and all of the faith one exercises, will literally be fulfilled because it will be the will of God. Your challenge is to learn as quickly as possible how to determine what the Spirit is whispering to you.

Learning to recognize answers to our prayers is yet another area where practice will improve proficiency. A chapter will be devoted to answers to prayers later in the book. As you ponder what a missionary is expected to do and be, you will become aware of many more areas that need serious attention. If you make the mistake of believing that you can wait until you arrive at the MTC before seriously beginning your preparation, you may find that your decision has cost you the privilege of serving a full time mission. At least, your lack of preparation will result in hours, days, weeks, and months of anguished catching up. Do yourself a favor and prepare now for what can be the greatest experience of your life, to this point — a full time mission.

*Chapter 3*

# START EARLY – AVOID MISTAKES

In the November 2002 general conference a new battle cry was introduced: "Raise the bar!" Since that time many of the general authorities have taken up the theme. In December 2002 a letter was issued by the First Presidency outlining in some detail the direction that "raising the bar" was to take. As bishops and stake presidents began to implement the newly emphasized standards, there were many disappointed young people who had slipped off the "straight and narrow path," repented, and planned on serving missions. The reality began to sink in when they were painfully informed that because of their past behavior, they would have to find an alternate way of serving because a full-time mission was no longer an option.

Yet another of the adversary's deceptive tactics is to whisper to young Latter-day Saints that they can act, dress, recreate, do drugs, be immoral, indulge in forbidden recreation like their counterparts in the world, and a thousand other things and still qualify for all the blessings promised to the righteous. Nephi saw our day and lamented: "and thus the devil cheateth their souls, and leadeth them away carefully down to hell" (2 Nephi 28:21). I have been in the adjacent office and heard the wailing when a young man discovered, too late, that he couldn't qualify for a full-time mission. What a tragedy. After an eternity of faithfulness in the pre-earth life, to be hoodwinked into believing that he could pick up the end of the stick labeled "the world" and not get what is inescapably on the other end of the stick — which isn't a full-time mission.

To add yet another voice to those of the prophets, I would raise the following warning flag. If you are wise, you'll not assume that what has been said and written really isn't the way things are, that you can beat the system, or that you are the exception to the rule. Be wise enough to "learn with joy and not with sorrow" (Jacob 4:3).

In the last ten years there have been three monumental letters published, clearly setting forth the standards for those planning on serving full time missions. One was issued on March 4, 1993 (while I was serving as mission president). The second letter, issued June 19, 1998, reinforced the first and clarified the church's resolve to have worthy, qualified missionaries representing the Savior and His church. The most recent letter, dated December 11, 2002, took a more hard line approach to worthiness and re-emphasized the need for preparation — especially being prepared to serve and teach with the Lord's Spirit. Those missionaries who are now preparing to leave on their missions were just little boys when the first letter was issued. Sufficient time has lapsed that those in the pipeline should have been warned, taught, and counseled to avoid mission-threatening activities and behaviors.

No matter your age when reading this book, it would be wise to make an appointment with your bishop or branch president and ask them to carefully go over the entire December

11, 2002 letter. If there are areas that need correcting, don't mistakenly believe that you can postpone repentance until you are eighteen, then see the bishop, get your hands slapped, and be prepared to serve when nineteen.

It might be to your advantage to ask the bishop or stake president to give a youth fireside going over the temple recommend questions one at a time and explaining what they mean. Before you are sent to the MTC you take out your temple endowments. If you conduct yourself so that you are worthy and prepared to enter the temple, you are more likely worthy to be a full time missionary. The idea of "sin now, repent later, and still be worthy to serve" is a tactic of the adversary that may have worked in the past but, given the world in which we live, is not acceptable in today's world. The reason for the "raising of the bar" is to help you, the missionary, qualify for the needed guidance and protection of the Holy Ghost to insure your protection and success.

What areas pose the greatest threat to you serving? Interestingly, in March of 1993 "emotional stability" (or the lack thereof) was the number one reason a young applicant was disqualified. The number two reason a prospective missionary was not allowed to serve was "moral worthiness" (or again, the lack thereof). By 1998 "moral worthiness" had taken the number one spot and "emotional stability" had slipped to the number two spot.

If we take the positioning of the "issues that disqualify" as an indication of where Satan is focusing his efforts to destroy young people, then the first warning flag ought to center around staying morally clean and worthy to serve. Immorality doesn't just happen. President David O. McKay wisely counseled: "Tell me what you think about when you do not have to think, and I will tell you what you are. Temptation does not come to those who have not thought of it before. Keep your thoughts clean, and it will be easy to resist temptations as they come" (*Gospel Interpretations*, page 401).

If you are really sincere about avoiding the deceptive tactics of the adversary, then you'll evaluate what methods Satan is using to get you to focus on immoral thoughts. When viewed from that perspective it becomes glaringly obvious that the devil is into media clear up past his eyes. It is impossible to listen to the warnings and counsels from the Brethren and not realize that pornography, in any form, is not innocent, is poison, and will destroy you just as surely as drugs will destroy the addict.

A young man from one of my Missionary Preparation classes at BYU sent me an e-mail asking for advice on how he could help his returned missionary roommates see that rated R movies were not condoned by the Church. Their argument was that the Brethren are no longer saying "don't watch rated R movies" and therefore we should be left to ourselves to choose what to watch and what not to watch. One wonders if these young returned missionaries have any clue what they are saying. Can they really be sufficiently deaf (spiritually and physically) that they can't hear the Brethren repeated raise the warning voice against "sleaze", "pornography in any form," "anything that excites the passions in an immoral way," and the list goes on and on. Those who are serious about preparing for the Celestial Kingdom have no lack of prophetic direction to keep them from being blindsided by the devil.

It might be worth pausing a moment to see the God-revealed consequences of looking and lusting. "And verily I say unto you, as I have said before, he that looketh on a woman to lust after her, or if any shall commit adultery in their hearts, they shall not have the Spirit, but shall deny the faith and shall fear" (D&C 63:16). The "as I have said before" refers to the Lord's stern warning in Doctrine and Covenants 42:23 where the Lord added this warning: "and if he repents not he shall be cast out." Note carefully the inescapable results of looking at pornography and lusting after the men or women (and regrettably, children) who are prostituted there.

1. **They shall not have the Spirit.** In missionary work the Spirit is absolutely essential. Without the Spirit you cannot teach (see D&C 42:14). As we'll see in a later chapter, without the Spirit you cannot stand against the devil in the last days. When the Spirit withdraws, one's "mind is darkened" (see D&C 10:2). It would be frightening to list what the scriptures say are the consequences of losing the Spirit.

2. **They shall deny the faith.** It isn't long, following the Spirit's withdrawal, that the unrepentant person starts to argue with the Lord and His prophets as to the wisdom and relevance of the commandments and the directives given by the Lord's mouthpiece. Before long the person without the Spirit begins to criticize the leaders of the church. Joseph Smith outlined the next spiritually fatal step:

> "I will give you one of the Keys of the mysteries of the Kingdom. It is an eternal principle, that has existed with God from all eternity: That man who rises up to condemn other, finding fault with the Church, saying that they are out of the way, while he himself is righteous, then know assuredly, that that man is in the high road to apostasy; and if he does not repent, will apostatize, as God lives." (*Teachings of the Prophet Joseph Smith*, p.156)

3. **They shall fear.** This may not happen until years later when, having lost their membership in the Church, and in many cases their mates and children, now hopeless and far from being a candidate for the Celestial Kingdom, abandoned by Satan (because he feels he has secured them and can focus his destructive efforts on others), they begin to fear that their chances for Eternal Life have evaporated forever. What a sorry state.

If you or anyone you know is viewing pornography and rationalizing that it is "innocent fun," then listen to what the scriptures and the prophets are saying. Because this has become such a destructive monster, listen to what Isaiah said when he saw our day — perhaps even the movies and DVDs we would be tempted to watch. "The sinners in Zion are afraid; fearfulness hath surprised the hypocrites. Who among us shall dwell with the devouring fire? Who among us shall dwell with everlasting burnings?

He that walketh righteously, and speaketh uprightly;... that stoppeth his ears from hearing of blood, and shutteth his eyes from seeing evil" (Isaiah 33:14-15). Looking a little closer at the scripture, and asking questions that bring understanding we ask, who will be afraid? Those in Zion who are sinning. Who will be eaten up with fearfulness? Those who are hypocrites — they say one thing and do another. They appear to be one thing on Sunday and are entirely different during the week or when out with their friends. "Who among us shall dwell with the devouring fire?" The description of when the Savior comes again at the Second Coming is described as "devouring fire," so Isaiah seems to be asking, "who is going to make it through the Second Coming without being burned up?" "Who among us shall dwell with everlasting burnings?" God dwells in everlasting burnings, so Isaiah seems to be asking, "who will eventually be able to live with God in His Celestial Kingdom?" His answer (and we'll only take the last two that he mentions): he that "stoppeth his ears from hearing of blood, and shutteth his eyes from seeing evil." Can the violence so prevalent in today's movies and DVD be any more accurately described than "blood"? Can "seeing evil" be any plainer than the watching of pornography? So it seems evident, if you don't want to burn at the Second Coming and you want to live with God in the Celestial Kingdom, you'd better conscientiously avoid pornography and violent movies — exactly what our prophet leaders have been counseling us for many years.

Our leaders have continually warned us against any kind of sexual stimulation before marriage. It isn't easy, but it is absolutely necessary, if you are going to spiritually prepare for a mission, that you control those good and God-given urges which are only to be used in marriage. Any unauthorized expressions of your sexuality put in jeopardy your opportunity to serve a mission.

Life today is like living on a roller coaster. Its ups and downs can be difficult to manage. However, compared to the emotional roller coaster of a mission, what you are going through now is fairly tranquil and smooth. You must learn to control your mood swings now. If that requires counseling and medication (usually it does not), then you'd better get the help you need. It isn't realistic to believe you can "throw a temper tantrum" or "lose your cool" at home or with your friends and then think you'll have perfect control in the mission field. Consider that whatever you are tempted with here at home will be ten times as difficult in the mission field. Don't disqualify yourself from mission-ary service because you haven't taken the steps to control your temper during these preparation years.

If you have fallen into the satanic trap of drug abuse, do whatever is necessary to break free. Get counseling, therapy, help from parents, priesthood leaders, and friends. What a terrible disappointment to find that what started out as mere teenage curiosity, ended up in a mission-disqualifying addiction. Satan has become so vicious in these last days that when Peter, the ancient apostle, saw our day, he said: "Be sober, be vigilant; because your adversary the devil, as a roaring lion, walketh about, seeking whom he may devour" (1 Peter 5:8).

So many youth, even those who claim membership in the Church, have taken a very irresponsible stance towards keeping the laws of the land. A little shoplifting, an attempt to outrun the police, a little vandalism, some mindless graffiti, an unpaid traffic ticket, a misdemeanor on your record, or any of a hundred other "teenage pranks" can disqualify you from serving a mission. A generation or two ago it wasn't a big thing if a kid had a brush with the law. Now the same thing can result in juvenile detention and then years of probation. One cannot serve while on parole or on legal probation. Be warned — beware!!

If current trends continue, you will be the exception rather than the rule if you make it through your teenage years without a permanent blemish on your police record. If you will immerse yourself in Church related activities, with friends who have a similar goal of serving a mission and refuse to engage in any mission-destroying activity — or even if you have to stand alone — then you'll make it through fine. If you stray one inch onto the devil's side of the line, then you are in serious trouble. You may choose to take the first step into the devil's territory, but you can never calculate where you will end up. One night with the wrong crowd in the wrong place at the wrong time could result in your committing a death-penalty crime and being sentenced to "life in prison, without parole" — it happened to a friend of ours!

Contracting the HIV virus may also preclude you from serving a mission. It seems like the list of ways and conditions that could jeopardize your mission could get longer and longer with no end in sight. Perhaps asking a couple of questions with a principle in mind would be more effective in helping you avoid mission-threatening problems.

Ask yourself, "If I do this, will it put a question mark over my worthiness to serve?" If the answer is "yes," run like you would from a wildfire.

Ask yourself, "Will this activity help me better prepare for a mission?" If the answer is "no," then don't do it.

The principle is: "Anything that takes me off the straight and narrow path leading to the Celestial Kingdom is not worth doing and should be avoided." Just applying that one principle would simplify the decisions you must make in order to look back on your mortal existence without regret. Start right now and resolve to live one day at a time, doing the best you can, repenting immediately whenever you slip off the straight and narrow path, be as diligent as you can in preparing, and you're poised to be a successful missionary.

*Chapter 4*

# TAKING ADVANTAGE OF YOUR TEENAGE YEARS

The teenage years are the golden years of preparation for the rest of your life. They are the fun, carefree years before mission, college, marriage, and beginning life's career. However, they are also the years which seem to separate "the men from the boys" or "the women from the girls." Not taking these years seriously can signal trouble ahead.

We don't know very much about Jesus' growing up years. Luke records: "And Jesus increased in wisdom and stature, and in favour with God and man" (Luke 2:52). In that one short verse the Savior modeled for us the perfect use of our teenage years.

**First, Jesus increased in "wisdom"** — *intellectually.* Given all of the opportunities we have to learn, I can't think of a valid excuse if we get to the final judgment and are found lacking intellectually. As adult-like as it may seem, the sooner you can resolve to be serious about your intellectual growth, the further ahead you'll be when the time for your mission arrives.

Particularly since the church is now in most of the

countries of the world and the gospel is being taught in every major language and many minor, seldom heard of languages, it would be wise to take as many language courses as possible in junior high and high school. What an advantage if you have learned how to learn languages and you receive a call to teach the gospel in a foreign language. Let me quickly state that just because you've taken five years of Spanish doesn't mean you'll be called to a Spanish-speaking mission. We had a young man assigned to our mission who spoke six languages fluently and was called to teach the gospel in English. Many others had put on their missionary recommendation forms that they didn't want to learn a language, but they were assigned to foreign language speaking missions. The Lord is in charge and He'll use you wherever He knows you'll be most effective.

Any familiarity you develop with different customs and cultures will only make your transition into mission life that much easier. Just being culturally sensitive is a huge step in the right direction. The church has been embarrassed several times and the missionary work has been halted for long periods of time because insensitive missionaries have failed to learn to respect the customs and cultures of the peoples they were serving.

A knowledge of history demonstrates that you are not just a mindless teenager. Additionally, history really does seem to repeat itself. Knowing the migrations of the different peoples of the world may help you understand some of their core beliefs. When I started to understand the plight of the Hmong and Lao refugees living in our mission, my empathy for them and my understanding of how to best meet their needs skyrocketed. When I came to understand the symbolism of their art and jewelry, I was even more convinced that their ancestors may have been visited by the Resurrected Savior. We don't yet have the record, but we will eventually.

Don't be afraid to challenge yourself. Take courses you know nothing about. You may discover your life's passion in an area in which you are not currently conversant. Become a gospel scholar as well. Don't be satisfied with a superficial understanding of the doctrine of the church. If you think you know everything that the Lord has revealed, you are dead wrong. After serving a two and a half year mission in Samoa, serving twice as a stake mission president, once as a mission president, and teaching the gospel professionally for over thirty years, there is one thing I know for sure — compared to what there is to know, I know absolutely nothing! I have never met a preparing or serving missionary who "knows it all." I have met many who think they do! Keep learning, keep growing intellectually, keep increasing in wisdom and knowledge, and you'll be fulfilling the Lord's invitation to become "even as I am" (see 3 Nephi 27:27).

**Second, Jesus increased in stature — *physically.*** One of the disturbing trends in America is the obesity of young people. Because we are a "sit in front of the televison or computer" generation, it is more difficult to get in shape and stay in shape. Missions are not easy. It will require all the strength and stamina you can muster to meet the challenges of the mission. Several times during my mission to Samoa, my life was literally saved because I was in good physical shape. One time the outrigger canoe we were riding in between the inter-island boat and the beach capsized while coming across the reef. Both my companion and I were thrown out into a small rip-tide. Immediately my companion was swept a hundred yards out into the ocean. I managed to get onto the protruding reef. Seeing that he was in serious trouble, I dove off the reef and swam to his rescue. It was fairly easy getting to him, as I was carried by the same current which dragged him away from shore. The challenge came when I tried to tow him back to shore. Now fighting against the flow of the current, it was all I could do to keep myself going. He wasn't in as good shape as I was, so he wasn't able to help much. Thanks to the physical conditioning I had endured as a football player and high school wrestler and the knowledge I had gained earning my Swimming and Life Saving merit badges, I was able to tow him to the protruding reef where the local people helped us get to shore.

The "unauthorized" swim wasn't a planned event. Accidents and emergencies seldom are! When the call for action comes, it is too late to start your preparation. You will be light-years ahead if you get in and stay in good physical shape. That includes learning to eat right, get adequate rest, and regular exercise.

Those who are in good physical condition are less likely to spend much "down time" sick or injured. This would be a great time to seriously look yourself over in the mirror. If changes need to be made so that your lack of physical preparation does not hamper the work, then make the change. Excuses are "a dime a dozen," but they won't compensate for failure to prepare physically. A principle I have seen in action in many areas of life is: "If you really want to do something, you'll find a way. Otherwise you'll find an excuse!" No excuse will do when it comes to serving the Lord with all your "might and strength"!

**Third, Jesus increased in "favor with God"** — *spiritually.* Spirituality is defined for this purpose as your relationship with God. By doing what God commanded, Jesus increased in favor with His Father. We can do the same. None of us is perfect, but that doesn't excuse us from trying to be the best we can.

There are many areas that you can become perfect in right now. President Spencer W. Kimball taught that we can become perfect a little bit at a time (*Teachings of Spencer W. Kimball* page 536). We can pay a perfect tithing, live the

Word of Wisdom perfectly. We can be perfect in our Sabbath Day observance. We can be perfect in not swearing or watching pornographic movies. We can be perfect in saying our prayers every night and morning. We can be perfect in reading our scriptures daily. Start with where you are and consciously strive to increase in spirituality.

Before you enter the MTC, you will be permitted to enter the temple and take out your endowment. There you will be taught (symbolically) how to become perfect. You won't glean all there is in the endowment the first time you go through. It will take many, many years of pondering and meditating before the endowment will yield many of its secrets. Just be patient.

Getting on a schedule of reading the scriptures daily will keep you in touch with what is eternally important. Daily prayer will keep you focused on God and Eternal Life. I have never met a person who apostatized from the church who was praying and reading the scriptures daily. In fact, you can almost use prayer and scripture reading as a thermometer to take your spiritual temperature. The less you read and pray, the lower your spiritual temperature will be. If you fail to read and pray long enough you run the risk of dying of spiritual hypothermia.

Attending to all your church meetings seems like a reasonable thing to do because you're going to be inviting your investigators to become fully active in the church. It would be total hypocrisy to ask others to do what you do not do yourself. The more you become accustomed to attending all your meetings each Sunday, the easier will be the transition if you have to attend six or even nine hours of meetings each Sunday because you are assigned to work in several wards.

Pay an honest tithe now — it will empower your testimony while serving your mission. After a young elder had given one of the finest talks I had ever heard on tithing at one of our zone conferences, he was being congratulated by his fellow missionaries. He finally came up to me, I assume to receive my commendation. I commended him on his talk and then said: "That was probably the finest talk I've ever heard on tithing except for one thing." He questioned what that one thing was. I said, "You didn't pay your tithing before coming on a mission, did you?" He was startled and admitted that he hadn't. Then he questioned how I knew. I said, "Because as you spoke the Spirit didn't bear witness to me that you were speaking as a living witness. Virtually everything you said was true except the most vital testimony of all — that of a personal testimony." I think I learned as much from that experience as he did. You can't testify with the same power about things you don't know and haven't lived as those who do know and are living the principles.

For your future benefit start now to gain a personal testimony of each and every principle of the gospel. Then when you are called upon to teach and testify, the Spirit will convey the truth of what you are saying unto the heart of the investigator which such power that they can no longer excuse themselves as "never having heard."

**Fourth, Jesus increased in favor with man — *socially*.** If it weren't so pathetic, it would be funny to see how many prospective missionaries try to escape learning the social skills that will make them successful as missionaries, in marriage, and in life. I know it can be a bit intimidating to talk to a college professor when you are a cowering freshman. So many of my students look at the floor when they talk to me. It can be unnerving to talk with the stake president or bishop when you are a lowly beehive or deacon. However, if you are going to be an able representative of the Savior, you must learn how to project yourself in a socially acceptable manner.

Too often we become so engrossed in what we are doing

that we are unaware of what we are really doing. An elder called me one day and asked for help with his junior companion. It seems that the junior companion would become extremely nervous when teaching. Unconsciously he would pick his nose and flip it. I suggested that the senior companion could bring the problem to his companion's attention and that should cure the problem. He responded that he had tried to teach his companion but without success.

I told him I would handle the problem in my own way. I had recently spoken in the sacrament meeting of the ward where the two missionaries were serving and had jokingly told the bishop that he "owed me one" to which he said I could have "even to the half of my kingdom." I called the bishop and ask if he would do me a favor, to which he responded in the affirmative. I told him the problem and asked if he would mind inviting the missionaries over for dinner then have them teach a discussion to his family. He agreed. I said, "If the problem arises, will you and your family find a way of bringing it to the junior companion's attention?" He said he would. The next day I received a call from the bishop. Laughingly he told what happened.

As the discussion started the senior companion gave the first principle and then turned the time to his junior companion. As the junior started his presentation, he became nervous and begin to pick his nose and flip it. At first the mother did a quick ducking motion. The junior companion looked at her rather strangely but went on. Next the bishop performed the ducking motion. Again the junior companion paused and looked at him questioningly. Before long each of the kids were doing the same ducking motion. Finally the junior companion stopped and ask if anything was wrong. The mother responded: "No, not really. We are trying to concentrate on what you are saying but it is difficult when you keep flipping boogers at us!" That cured the junior companion immediately.

Each of us have little habits, called "tics," which we do unconsciously but which are distracting or even irritating to those we are teaching. What an advantage you would have if you would be humble and teachable enough to identify and overcome those "tics" before being called to the mission field.

Most people are forgiving and understanding, but with a little practice, we don't have to rely upon their forgiving, understanding natures to accommodate our tics. Sometimes it is saying "ah" between every word. Sometimes it is saying something like "you know what I mean?" after each statement. It might be calling people "dude" or some other trendy name. All of these may be acceptable in your social circle at home but may constitute a "turn off" to the people we are trying to teach. For a great many people, it doesn't take much of a "turn off" to give them the excuse not to listen to you and your precious message.

You shouldn't need to be forced to interface with adults and people of education and status. You can learn to be socially sensitive without being obnoxious or overbearing. You can learn when to leave after a short visit and not over-stay your welcome. You can practice your social skills at the table, during family visits, when you visit your friends' homes and interact with their parents. Limitless are the opportunities for you to become like Jesus by becoming socially acceptable.

You might ask, "could God put me into a position of leadership without being afraid that I would drive the people I am called to lead away from the Church?" If you are honest in your answer, you'll know how far you have to go before becoming like Jesus in this vital area.

Many times it isn't "what" you say that makes the difference whether you're accepted or rejected. It is "how" you say it that makes the difference. Practice watching closely as you make comments, whether people shy away from you or willingly engage you in conversation. If they shy away, then modify your approach. Try several methods of phrasing and rephrasing your questions or comments. Watch carefully how you interject your comments into the conversation. Do you rudely interrupt? Do you make too many comments in classes? Do you expect others to carry the conversation while you sit by and say nothing? Do you listen intently as others speak? Do you feel that what you have to say is more important than what anyone else can say?

These are just a few of the questions that will help you get a handle on how you are doing socially. If it weren't vitally important that you be well balanced in all four of these areas, I seriously doubt that God would have inspired Luke to give us the one single-verse insight on how Christ became the Perfect Man. Now our challenge is to become like Him in all areas. Don't be discouraged when you stumble and fail — often. Just keep trying. It will take longer than a lifetime in order for you to become totally Christlike. Just enjoy the process of knocking off the rough edges and polishing yourself in each of these four Christlike areas.

*Chapter 5*

# REPENTANCE – WHY AND HOW?
# PART 1: CONFESSION

In each of the chapters in this book dealing with doctrine, there will be a two-fold purpose. First, to teach you so you can apply the principles in your own life. It is my hope that by showing you the "Big Picture" you can see how each part of the gospel fits perfectly with every other part. Secondly, it is my hope that I can teach you with such clarity and simplicity that you, in turn, can teach the thousands of our Father's children who are now being prepared by the Spirit to receive the gospel at your hands.

Paul taught: "For all have sinned, and come short of the glory of God" (Romans 3:23). That probably isn't a revelation to anyone. There has only been one Perfect Person who ever lived on the face of the Earth and that was the Savior. So when we talk about repentance, no one is being singled out. It is something that virtually every human being, from the president of the church to the lowliest person on earth, needs. I am going to try to teach about repentance with a series of questions which I will pose and answers from the scriptures and from many years of experience as a priesthood leader.

45

Why do we need to repent? Isaiah 59:2 states: "But your iniquities have separated between you and your God, and your sins have hid his face from you, that he will not hear." Any time that a person sins (i.e. willfully transgresses the laws of God), then they are disqualified from being in the presence of God. Nephi taught: "Wherefore, if ye have sought to do wickedly in the days of your probation, then ye are found unclean before the judgment-seat of God; and no unclean thing can dwell with God; wherefore, ye must be cast off forever" (1 Nephi 10:21).

No rational being wants to be eternally shut out from the presence of God. So how can we become "clean" again so we can inherit the Kingdom of God? That is where repentance comes into play. We will not discuss the "5 R's of Repentance," although they are instructive and valuable. We will take the simple mathematical formula given by the Lord, the application of which brings the desired forgiveness.

In Doctrine and Covenants 58:42-43 the Lord states: "Behold, he who has repented of his sins, the same is forgiven, and I, the Lord, remember them no more.

"By this ye may know if a man repenteth of his sins — behold, he will confess them and forsake them." So if a person: 1) confesses + 2) forsakes = Forgiven and (p.s.) God remembers no more. Will you still remember after you have been forgiven? Yes! Why? Most of us recognize the value of the pain, the disappointment, the feelings of self-betrayal, the regret that are associated with remembering our past sins. Those painful memories keep us from re-committing the sin. Will there ever come a time during mortal life when we will "remember them no more"? Many of you may be young enough not to know the answer to that question. The answer (at least in my own case and those older people I have talked with) is "yes." After the Lord sees that it is no longer necessary for the memory of past transgressions to stop you from committing the sin again, He can and will erase them from your memory. If He has chosen not to blot out the memory of your sins yet, be patient. If you continue faithful, He eventually will. "Now the Spirit knoweth all things; nevertheless the Son of God suffereth according to the flesh that he might take upon him the sins of his people, that **he might blot out their transgressions according to the power of his deliverance**; and now behold, this is the testimony which is in me" (Alma 7:13, emphasis added).

So how do we attain that blessed state where God will forgive and remember our sins no more? First, we must confess. Why must we confess? The most compelling reason is: because God commanded us to! It is the Lord who dictates the conditions on which He will forgive our sins — not us. Over the many years I have served as a priesthood leader and a religion teacher, I have encountered many people who try to prescribe to God what they will do and what they won't do in order to get forgiveness. That never did and never will work. We need to seek to understand His commandments and voluntarily comply, or the promised blessings will not be forthcoming.

While I was serving as a mission president, my assistants would occasionally become agitated at me when I knew that certain missionaries were breaking the mission rules and I didn't "nail them" immediately. The assistants wanted to know why I didn't confront them concerning their disobedience. I told them I didn't because I wanted to give the missionaries the opportunity to repent. Then I explained that the Lord never did say He would forgive if they "admitted and forsook" their sins. The difference, as I understand it, between "admitting" and "confessing" is that while admitting involves being caught or confronted with your sinful behavior, confessing is a voluntary coming forth — without being caught.

My experience has been that "admitting" can often lead to

"confessing," but in the absence of coming forth voluntarily, the repentance process is dramatically slowed, if not halted altogether. If you want to be forgiven, then you need to see your priesthood leader, even if you are never caught.

Many years ago while I taught seminary, students would ask: "Brother Bott, how far can we go on our dates before we have to talk with the bishop?" I would answer: "I wouldn't go see the bishop. That would be really embarrassing!" They knew I was leading them along but weren't quite experienced enough to see where I was taking them. They would warily ask: "Why wouldn't you confess to the bishop?" I would say, "I wouldn't confess unless I wanted to be forgiven of my sins!" Then I would discuss with them the principle of confession.

Since our sins separate us from our God (remember Isaiah 59:2), then whenever we sin the Lord signalizes His disapproval by partially withdrawing His Spirit (I say partially because if He altogether withdrew His Spirit we would die — see D&C 88:13). When the Spirit leaves, the internal peace leaves with it. We live in a world where turmoil is swirling around us all the time. We can stand that because we have that inner peace from God "which passeth all understanding" (see Philippians 4:7). When we sin, the turmoil and spiritual darkness which surrounds us moves in to fill the inner gap as the Spirit withdraws. We hate that empty, dark, abandoned feeling and want the comforting influence of the Spirit back in our lives. That causes us to want to repent.

The first thing we do is kneel down and ask for God's forgiveness. How do we know if He has accepted our repentance as sufficient? It is easy — the Spirit and the inner peace return! God said: "And the place where it is my will that you should tarry, for the main, shall be signalized unto you by the peace and power of my Spirit, that shall flow unto you" (D&C 111:8). So when we are where the Lord wants us to be (in the main — not specifically, but heading in the right direction), He will signalize it by peace and power of the Spirit. That is also what it means when the scriptures say "by the Spirit ye are justified" (see Moses 6:60). Being "just" or "justified" means that you are without blame before God or not under Divine condemnation. Not that you're perfect but that you are doing as well as the Lord expects you to given the amount of light and knowledge He has revealed to you. And you also have the promise that if you will continue living in the Spirit, no matter where you are on the pathway to perfection when you die, you will be allowed to continue until you attain the highest degree of the Celestial Kingdom. If the peace and Spirit return, you have satisfied Divine requirements and you need go no further as far as confession is concerned.

If the Spirit and peace do not return after you have confessed to God, then you must find the person you have wronged and ask for their forgiveness. There may be instances where seeking forgiveness from the offended actually does more harm in re-opening old wounds than remaining silent would do. Consult your priesthood leader on the proper course of action. Whether they forgive you or not is not the major issue — that is between them and God (see D&C 64:8-11). When you have done all you can do to make it right, then you'll know whether that is sufficient because the Spirit will come back into your life and the inner peace will return.

If the Spirit and peace do not return, then apparently you are too close to your transgression to see how to get from the sinful state you are in back to the desired state of enjoying the Spirit and peace. So, mercifully, God has provided a bishop, stake president, or mission president upon whom He has bestowed the keys of judgment, to help you figure out what you have to do to gain forgiveness. The bishop, stake president or mission president does not forgive sins.

That is reserved for a very select few on the earth (see Miracle of Forgiveness pp 332-33). The priesthood leader can, after you have fully disclosed the transgression, prescribe by revelation or impressions which come from the Spirit, what you must do to gain forgiveness.

Won't the bishop think less of me when I tell him what I've done? Just the opposite. Contrary to popular belief, most bishops were young once. They know how much courage it takes to confess sins. So instead of dimishing, you actually increase in their eyes.

Won't the bishop think of my past sins every times he sees me? I relearned one of the great lessons of life early in my tenure as a mission president. A significant number of the missionaries I inherited when I began my service as a mission president had decided to wait until the new president arrived before clearing up past transgressions. By the time I finished interviewing the missionaries and listening to their belated confessions, I thought I was the president of the Sodom and Gomorrah Mission. I had promised the missionaries that, if they would come clean with past transgressions, they would take off spiritually in a way they had never experienced in their entire lives. I knew that was true because un-repented sin is like a heavy weight around your neck. You can swim across the lake of life on the surface and it is pretty nice, but twelve feet below the surface it isn't so pleasant.

One elder called and said: "President, it is just like you said, everyone is really taking off spiritually, but I'm not. I wasn't totally honest with you when we had our interview. Could we meet again and take care of the rest of it?" I agreed and met him at his apartment. He asked: "Do you remember the last time we met?" I said "yes" and told him the building we had met in and the room in that building. He seemed pleased that I would remember. Then he asked: "Do you remember what we talked about?" To my horror I couldn't remember. I said a quick, silent prayer "Dear Heavenly Father, this isn't very funny. If You take away my mind this early on in my presidency, I'll never find my way back to the mission home!" I told him I couldn't remember. He looked really hurt and asked if I really didn't care about him. I cared, but I couldn't remember. I said, "I'm sorry, you'll just have to tell me again what we talked about." He got about two sentences into the re-confession and the whole story came back. I said, "That's enough. I remember now. You can go on."

On the way back to the mission home I was complaining a little to the Lord when it felt like someone lifted up the top of my head, poured in a quart of inspiration, and slammed the lid down. It was like someone said: "Dear President Bott, don't you realize that in the repentance process you represent Me. If, after a person has confessed and forsaken, I God, the Greatest of all, remember it no more, who do you think you are that you should still remember?" I was thrilled. I told the missionaries that if they were going to re-confess a sin, they would have to remind me. That is the blessing God gives priesthood leaders to help them sleep.

How much do I have to confess? Un-repented sin is like an infected sore. If you clean out half of the infection and cover it over, what happens? Obviously, it reinfects and is often worse than the original sore. So when you confess, don't hold back. Dump out the entire contents of the sin bucket. Most priesthood leaders are not interested in hearing all the minute details of the transgression. They want to know the extent of the transgression so they can figuratively draw a perimeter around the sin to contain the spread of the infection.

Won't the bishop tell others and they in turn spread it around the ward? This is one of the common misconceptions among uninformed members of the Church. The priesthood leader is under what is called the

"Priest/Penitent Act." That is a legal act which states that without your permission the "priest" (or for Latter-day Saints, the bishop, stake president, or mission president) is not authorized to share the content of your confession with anyone else — even at the peril of him being imprisoned! The priesthood leader may ask for your permission to share the general nature of your transgression with his counselors or the stake president for additional counsel on how to proceed or if a church disciplinary council is necessary.

In the many years I have served in bishoprics and stake presidencies and as a mission president, I have never seen that confidence broken. I have heard a lot of stories about broken confidences, but when followed to their source, the stories either are not true or the transgressors themselves have been the source of the "leak." Since we are human, I would assume there are occasional breaches of confidence by priesthood leaders, but they are so rare that the transgressor can confess to the priesthood leader and know that their confession will remain with that leader.

What will be the result of my completing the repentance process, which includes confessing? When the Lord lifts the burden of sin off your shoulders, you'll feel better than you have felt since the transgression. Unresolved sin crushes an individual's spirit. It destroys hope and leaves one feeling worthless and in despair. When the Lord "heals" your soul, the most frequently asked question is: "Why did I wait so long?" Once you have felt that healing power in your own life, you are more anxious to share with everyone you meet the knowledge of how to receive that forgiveness .

One of the more graphic illustrations of this desire to share the forgiveness they had experienced is the story of the sons of King Mosiah. Mormon records:

Now they were desirous that salvation should be declared to every creature, for they could not bear that any human soul should perish; yea, even the very thoughts that any soul should endure endless torment did cause them to quake and tremble.

And thus did the Spirit of the Lord work upon them, for they were the very vilest of sinners. And the Lord saw fit in his infinite mercy to spare them; nevertheless they suffered much anguish of soul because of their iniquities, suffering much and fearing that they should be cast off forever. (Mosiah 28:3-4)

Having experienced that forgiveness yourself, you will be infinitely more effective as a missionary. So why not take what steps are necessary to experience in your own life what I have written about? The single issue I deal with most as a teacher is getting my students, who have felt the Spirit and know they need to repent, to set an appointment with their bishops. If they wait to set the appointment they often talk themselves out of confessing. When the Spirit prompts, it is best to act immediately. So if the Spirit is whispering to you that you need to get some things cleared up, set the book down, pick up the phone, and call the bishop. Don't worry that it is late at night, early in the morning, or anytime during the day. He will be glad to set an appointment — one that will change your life forever.

*Chapter 6*

# REPENTANCE – WHY AND HOW?
# PART 2: FORSAKING
# AND FORGIVENESS

One would think that a discussion on forsaking sin would not be necessary. However, there are some key issues that seem to have escaped the attention of many of my students. The first question is: what does it mean to "forsake"? To stop doing what is wrong. There are two aspects of this: 1) forsake physically and 2) forsake mentally.

Repentance really means "turning away from." Since we do not live on a merry-go-round, the idea of sinning then repenting, with the thought of sinning again, is offensive to God. Joseph Smith taught: "Repentance is a thing that cannot be trifled with every day. Daily transgression and daily repentance is not that which is pleasing in the sight of God" (*Teachings of the Prophet Joseph Smith*, p.148). If you are serious about correcting mistakes made in your life, you must have the resolve never to sin again.

Is there a possibility that you will slip and make a

mistake again? Probably. In explaining the precarious situation the Nephites were in at the time of Christ birth, Mormon stated: "Now they did not sin ignorantly, for they knew the will of God concerning them, for it had been taught unto them; therefore **they did wilfully rebel** against God" (3 Nephi 6:18, emphasis added). A scripture that has always caused problems for those trying to repent, but finding that the way back to the straight and narrow path has been greased by the adversary, is Doctrine and Covenants 82:7, which reads: "And now, verily I say unto you, I, the Lord, will not lay any sin to your charge; go your ways and sin no more; but unto that soul who sinneth shall the former sins return, saith the Lord your God."

The key to understanding this verse is the definition of "sin." To that soul who willfully sins (or consciously turns back to his sinful ways), the former sins return. If the truly repentant person is blindsided by the adversary and, in a moment of weakness, unintentionally (without premeditation) falls back into forbidden pathways, do the former sins return? My understanding is that they do not. As long as we are diligently trying to become like God, even though we stumble and fall short, our former sins do not return. However, we cannot afford to trifle or play games with God. To say: "Oops! I goofed up again" when it was, in reality planned, will not escape the notice of the Omniscient One — it is impossible to deceive God!

The intent must be to forsake the sin and never, ever do it again. That may require changing friends, moving to a different environment, changing the recreational activities you are involved in, avoiding anything that reminds you of your sinful past. It is almost 100% sure, if Satan can lure a reformed alcoholic into a bar "just to be with his friends," that he will leave in a drunken state. The same is true of those who have used drugs, been involved sexually, etc. If you want to break the habit of sinful behavior, you have to move away from stimuli associated with your sinful past.

If Satan is successful in getting you to slip and fall again, don't be discouraged and give up. That is exactly what he wants you to do. He wants you to believe that you are too weak to overcome the sin, that you are hopelessly lost, that you are not the stuff the Celestial Kingdom is made of. That is why the Lord explains that Satan is a "liar from the beginning" (see D&C 93:25).

No matter how many times you have tried to quit, no matter how often you have fallen, no matter how many times you have vowed that you would never do it again and then did, it is never too late to try again. With the help of the Lord, you can overcome all things. He said: "For verily I say unto you, I will that ye should overcome the world; wherefore I will have compassion upon you" (D&C 64:2). Since it is His will that we overcome the world (or any weakness associated with the flesh), then surely He will help us succeed. That is exactly what He promised: "And if men come unto me I will show unto them their weakness. **I give unto men weakness** that they may be humble; and my grace is sufficient for all men that humble themselves before me; for if they humble themselves before me, and have faith in me, then will **I make weak things become strong unto them**" (Ether 12:27, emphasis added).

Rather than get discouraged because some weaknesses refuse to go away, why not do as Moroni suggested, humble yourself, exercise faith in Christ, go to Him in humble prayer, and allow Him to help you overcome all of your weaknesses? Start now with the resolve to never physically commit the sins that have plagued you — ever again.

Next we must resolve to forsake our sins mentally. That means don't think about them, don't talk about them, don't allow your mind to dwell on them. Too often missionaries want to share their sinful pasts with companions and others in the mission field. Sometimes in a bragging way, sometimes as a tool of teaching, sometimes in a mournful, regretful way. President Spencer W. Kimball counsels us not to do that:

> **Missionaries should not parade old sins**. As I have met with many groups of missionaries throughout the mission, I find a tendency for missionaries to tell their faults to their companions, their friends, and sometimes in public. There is not place in the mission field to publicize your weaknesses. When you have something that is disturbing you, you should go to your mission president. To him you may unburden yourself, confess your sins and your weaknesses. You may tell him your hopes and aspirations, but there is no reason why you should tell every companion the fact that you might have smoked a few cigarettes in your life before you came, or that you had taken the name of the Lord in vain, or any other of your weaknesses. We go forward on the assumption that you are worthy to do this work. If there is something of major importance in your life that had not been adjusted before your coming into the mission field, then certainly you should make those adjustments through your president. Don't tell the saints. That does not do anyone any good. It does not mean you are being hypocritical. You had some weaknesses, you repented, and those weaknesses are no longer a part of your life, and you are living in conformity with the program of the Church. (*The Teachings of Spencer W. Kimball*, p.96)

You will note that the Lord stated that after a person had confessed and forsaken his sins, then forgiveness would be forthcoming and that "God would remember it no more." Do we not run the risk of reminding God of our sins when we continue to talk about them? Could it be possible that in so reminding Him, we also temporarily undo the forgiveness He promised because we have not fully complied with His requirement to "forsake"? What a scary thought. Why run the risk of postponing forgiveness by talking about the forgiven past?

It might seem unnecessary to discuss what forgiveness is, but again, I have found with my college-age students that a majority seem to be lacking when it comes to understanding forgiveness. I would start with a statement and a question: "We know that sin throws the scales of eternal justice out of balance. What is it that balances the scales?" Almost always the answers I receive include "the atonement, mercy, repentance, etc." To which I answer: "Wrong!" That is more to get their attention so they don't miss the point. Actually they are only half wrong! In Alma 42, Alma explains to his errant son the relationship of justice to mercy. He states: "Now, repentance could not come unto men except there were a punishment" (Alma 42:16). So it is punishment that balances the scales of eternal justice. The reason their answers were only half right was because, unless there is sincere repentance, the suffering of the Savior does not satisfy the demands of justice. The Savior, Himself, said: "for behold, my blood shall not cleanse them if they hear me not" (D&C 29:17). He also explained: "For behold, I, God, have suffered these things for all, that they might not suffer if they would repent; But if they would not repent they must suffer even as I" (D&C 19:16-17).

For the unrepentant sinner, the only way the scales of eternal justice can be balanced is by his own personal suffering. Although we have quoted quite a few scriptures, there is another one that must be cited because your understanding of forgiveness is essential to your ability to teach the restored gospel. Alma further taught:

"Therefore, according to justice, the plan of redemption could not be brought about, only on conditions of repentance of men in this probationary state, yea, this preparatory state; for except it were for these conditions, mercy could not take effect except it should destroy the work of justice. Now the work of justice could not be destroyed; if so, God would cease to be God" (Alma 42:13). If mercy could rob justice, God would cease to be God! That isn't going to happen. So the ultimatum stands: "repent or suffer."

Now there are only two candidates to endure the suffering necessary to balance the scales of eternal justice: 1) the sinner; and 2) the Savior. If one repents, then the punishment (which must be exacted according to Eternal Law) is shifted to the Savior. If one chooses not to repent, then ultimately he will have to suffer. If the Savior's suffering in Gethsemane and on the Cross is applied to balance the scales of justice, then His Atonement pays the price and one is said to "have been forgiven."

Therefore, anything that is covered by the Atonement of Christ, following repentance, is said to be forgivable. To cement the concept in your mind, answer the following question: What are the three greatest sins a man can commit? The answer is: 1) Denying the Holy Ghost — which is the "unpardonable sin." 2) Murder — which, for a member of the church is the "unforgivable sin" (see D&C 42:18-19). 3) Sex sins — which (according to Alma 39:5-6) are "hard to be forgiven of."

Why are these three sins greater than any of the others? Because they all deal with a power which God lends to us on a temporary, trial basis — the power of life. Sexual sins represent the unauthorized "giving of life." Murder is the unauthorized "taking of life." Denying the Holy Ghost severs the lifeline between God and man while man is in a telestial state. Once that lifeline has been established and the heavens have been opened, and one knows by revelation and sure knowledge that the Plan of Salvation is true, then if he openly denies and defies the truth, that is like committing spiritual suicide.

Now the point: when God says that sexual sins are "hard to be forgiven of," He is saying that, although they are very serious, they do fall under the umbrella of the Atonement of Christ and therefore are "forgivable." Murder, however, for a member of the church is "unforgivable," meaning that the Atonement of Christ does not balance the scales of eternal justice — the murderer must pay — but apparently he can make the payment necessary to balance the scales. Therefore, murder for a member of the Church does not fall under the umbrella of the Atonement of Christ. Denying the Holy Ghost, which few men can do because of our lack of experience and knowledge, is "unpardonable," which means the Atonement of Christ doesn't pay for it, the guilty one cannot pay for it, therefore he is banished to Outer Darkness where he is eternally banished from the presence of God. Therefore, everyone in any of the three degrees of glory will be there because they are free from sin, either because they have repented and been forgiven, or because they have paid for their sins themselves. Thus the eternal scales of justice will be perfectly balanced and God will not cease to be God. Only the "Sons of Perdition" will remain filthy still and forever.

When I hear people rather flippantly say: "Oh, I can sin now and I'll repent later!" I wonder if they have any concept of what they are saying. In reality they are saying: "I can do whatever I want to and then I'll shift the punishment for my sins to the Savior when I get ready to quit sinning!" Then I hear them bear tearful testimony about how "Christ is my very best friend." I wonder what kind of a "friend" would willingly inflict suffering so intense and exquisite that it causes blood to come from every pure (see D&C 19:15-19) on their "very best friend"? Before you are prepared to teach the "Gospel of Repentance" (see D&C 13), you must understand the implications of sin and repentance. Forgiveness is not easy and it is not cheap. It cost the life of the Son of God!

Once forgiveness has been granted, you "crucify the old man of sin" (see Romans 6:3-6) and you literally become "a new creature in Christ" (see Mosiah 27:25-27). Now the new creature can confidently face the challenges of mortality without having to cower in the shadows because Satan will constantly dredge up the past and throw it endlessly in your face, trying to get you to feel you are not worthy to be a missionary or even a member of the Church.

If, after you have received the confirming witness that you have been forgiven (i.e. the Spirit has returned and that inner peace is back), you continue to re-identify yourself with the "old man of sin", then you are, in a sense, giving the adversary the bullets that he will subsequently use to destroy you.

When (not if) Satan throws your past in your face, you can confidently say: "Thank you Satan for reminding me what a wonderful blessing the Atonement of Christ really is. Now I am going to redouble my efforts in helping everyone I meet receive the same soul-healing forgiveness I have received. Get thee behind me, Satan!" and he will leave. If, however, he can drive a wedge between you and your confidence in your ability to keep the commandments, he will destroy you. You cannot afford to go into the mission field without knowing first-hand the cleansing, healing power of the Atonement.

When I was very young the teachers were still using a visual aid to teach repentance that was not accurate. They would bring in a board about two feet long. Then they would proceed to pound nails into the board explaining that this is what sin does to your soul. Then they would pull the nails out, explaining that this is what repentance does for you. What is wrong with that analogy? You'll readily see that the holes are still in the board. Is that what the Atonement does for you? Some might think that if we just putty and shellac the holes it will restore the board to its original condition. However, using an electron microscope the holes would be as readily observable as if they had never been filled. I believe the Atonement literally throws the old, pocked, marred board away and gives you a brand new one. What does the Atonement do for *you*?

My hope is that these two chapters on repentance will cause you to ponder, study, and pray about what the Atonement really means in your life. Since (as you will see in a later chapter) the Atonement is the hub or core of the entire gospel, without an understanding of the Atonement, your gospel wheel will never stand the jolts and bumps associated with your trek through the wilderness of mortality to the promised land in the Celestial Kingdom of God.

*Chapter 7*

# THE INTERVIEWS, THE CALL, THE ASSIGNMENT

Given the professional opportunity which I enjoy of teaching over two thousand preparing missionaries every year, I know the excitement which surrounds the mission call. There are many questions which underscore the anxiety associated with this time in your life. This chapter is intended to give some insight and advice that may help you through this wonderful time.

Of course you have been preparing for years, so when you begin filling out the papers is hardly the time to start preparing. However, even before you fill out the papers, it would be well to schedule three separate appointments with the health clinic to receive your Hepatitis A and Hepatitis B shots. If it has been over five years since you received a Tetanus booster, you will be required to get one. These shots are required no matter what mission you are assigned to. The catch comes that the Hepatitis shots must be spaced — one month between the first and second shot and six months between the first shot and the third shot. So if you are trying to get a head start on your medical preparation, plan now to get the shots.

You will almost certainly have to have your wisdom teeth extracted. Why not plan far enough ahead so that you can get them out at a time when you won't have to miss school or some other important function? It won't matter whether they are taken out a month or a year before you submit your papers.

You will need a complete physical exam by a medical doctor and a dental check-up by a dentist. If you crowd these too close to the time when you want to submit your papers, one or both of these professionals may not be immediately available and your scheduled appointment may delay your papers being complete so they can be submitted. The dental work must be done before the papers are submitted. If you are on any medication to stabilize your health — either physical or mental — you need to be confirmed stable and fully functional before submitting your papers. Rather than argue with the system, why not just decide to take whatever steps are necessary to comply?

If you know you are going to need corrective surgery before you can serve, get it scheduled well in advance so that any complications will not delay your call. If it has been some time since you had an eye examination or updated your glasses prescription, take care of that item on your "checklist of things to do."

Each missionary should have received his or her patriarchal blessing. It is strongly suggested that you get your missionary set of scriptures early enough to transfer any markings you may want to carry over from your seminary classes or other passages you have marked.

The more attention you can give to these issues, the less frustrating will be the completing of your Missionary Recommendation forms. You can submit your papers no earlier than ninety days from your availability date. Your availability date cannot be before your 19th birthday if you are an elder or your 21st birthday if you are a sister. Various ways have been tried to get around this rule — most have been totally unsuccessful. Why not resign yourself to play by the rules and not try to beat the system?

If you are planning on finishing the school year before going, but have already passed the minimum availability date (i.e. your birthday), then you must figure out when you want to go and calculate back ninety days from that date. In the thousands of pre-missionaries I have taught, there have only been a handful who were a) called before their availability date; or b) turned nineteen or twenty-one in the MTC. There have been a few, but not many!

Realize that the Brethren are dealing with over 60,000 missionaries — most of whom would like to get back in time to start Fall semester or "leave after our family reunion" or any of a thousand other reasons. If you are thoughtful, you'll see the tremendous pressure that puts on the missionary system to accommodate each individual missionary's particular desire. My counsel would be to put down your desire and then go with whatever the Brethren assign. The Lord is in control. He foreordained you to this very mission experience before the foundation of the world. Joseph Smith said, "Every man who has a calling to minister to the inhabitants of the world was ordained to that very purpose in the Grand Council of heaven before this world was" (*Teachings of the Prophet Joseph Smith*, p.365). God, Who is aware when a sparrow falls, and has all power and all knowledge, surely knows what your needs are and will (if you will allow Him) do what is eternally best for you.

Start your interviews early If there are problems to resolve, it may take some time. When you interview with the bishop, be open, honest, and forthcoming. Don't try to hide something in your past or believe you can lie to the bishop, get into the mission field, and take care of things later! That never has worked. If you think about it, you will see that lying to the bishop is like lying to God. Lying to get into the temple certainly will not entitle you to the endowment you need in order to be a successful missionary. If you lie to avoid an embarrassing delay, you are forfeiting your right to the Spirit, which will absolutely guarantee your failure as a missionary. The greatest favor you can do for yourself is to be totally honest in all of your interviews.

The bishop and/or stake president may ask you to go back and re-confess everything you have done in the past. There is real wisdom in this. Satan is going to dredge up everything you have ever done or said or thought, whether you have repented of it or not. It will happen. If he can make you feel unworthy to serve, you'll come home disgraced. He subtly works on you by saying something like: "Remember that one date? You didn't tell the bishop about that." Because, in the mission field you are striving harder to be perfect than you have ever tried before, you'll run in to confess to your mission president. Relief will come. A couple of weeks later, you'll hear another satanic voice saying, "OK, you took care of that one, but remember this other time?" He will run you ragged with what I call "confessionitus." By re-confessing everything you have ever done, *when* Satan throws your past in your face you can confidently say: "Well, if I didn't take care if it with the first bishop, I did with the second. Get thee behind me Satan!" and he will leave. The "re-confession" acts as a double insulating cover to protect you from the destructive efforts of the adversary. Use the opportunity — don't resent it.

If you need to postpone the start of your mission to complete the repentance process, then do it. You will be one hundred times better as a missionary who is worthy to serve than if you deceptively try to get into the mission field without repenting. If you don't get anything else out of this book, please realize that I am speaking from over three decades of experience and know the joy that comes when a young man or young woman serves worthily and I know the heartache and disappointment that comes when they try to serve without the Spirit.

After the bishop's interview there will be a stake president's interview. Many of the same questions will be asked. Just look at the interviews as the Lord's way of doubling and redoubling your insulated protective armor that you will use for the rest of your life against the destructive attacks by the adversary.

The generation into which you have been born seems to have grown up believing that you can say whatever you want to avoid the consequences of poor choices or to get whatever you want, whether you've earned it or not. Nothing could be more pleasing to the adversary, whose objective is to destroy your soul and make you miserable like unto to himself (see Moses 4:1-4 and 2 Nephi 2:18, 27).

Once all the paperwork is completed it usually takes between two and four weeks to receive the call. They can be the most nerve-wracking days of your life. However, you must remember that patience is a godly characteristic and you are going to have to learn it sooner or later. Don't call the Missionary Department bugging them about your call. However, if the call hasn't come within five weeks, you might want to ask your bishop or stake president to call and find the status of your papers. Sometimes the call hasn't been sent in, sometimes it has been lost or misplaced and without a replacement being sent, your mission call will never come.

As the days pass since the stake president submitted your papers, the excitement grows. Finally the call comes. If you are away attending school and submit your papers from your school address, you need to determine whether you want the call sent to your school address or your home address. It only delays the call by a few days if you have it sent to your school address and it doesn't arrive until after you've returned home. Just another detail to consider!

When you receive your call, and this is something I did not fully realize until I was called as a mission president, your **call is as a missionary**. It is separate and apart from your assignment. When President Hinckley called Sister Bott and me as mission president in late December, after accepting I innocently asked where we would be serving. He said: "Oh President Bott, this is a big, wonderful world. Where you serve really doesn't make that much difference. You may have your assignment changed four or five times before you end up where you'll eventually serve." Then he informed us that it would likely be about three more months before we got our assignment! Those were the longest three months we ever experienced. We had the "call" as mission president — that was the important part — but the assignment could change.

As a young missionary your call and your initial assignment come in the same letter, so it is natural to say: "I was called to such and such a mission." In reality, you were "called as a missionary for the Church of Jesus Christ of Latter-day Saints" and "your initial assignment is ..." If all young missionaries understood the difference, it would eliminate the worry and feelings of disappointing the Lord when circumstances dictate that you finish your mission somewhere other than where you started.

It was not uncommon for us to have missionaries who had served in Central or South America, became ill, returned home to recover, and then were re-assigned to complete their missions with us in California. Often it required several counseling sessions with them to help them see that 1) the Lord hadn't made a mistake in their initial assignment; 2) they hadn't disappointed the Lord; or

3) they were just as needed in the mission they have been reassigned to as they were in their initial mission.

So from the day you receive your call, adjust your thinking to reflect that you are called as a full-time missionary no matter where you are sent. You just happen to be needed initially in a certain mission or speaking a certain language. As you will not look at a transfer within your mission as a sign of failure, neither should you view a "super transfer" (one to an entirely new mission) as a sign of failure. Wouldn't it be great if the world were one huge mission? Then anywhere you were assigned to serve would be within that mission. I suspect if we saw things the way our Heavenly Father does, you would see that not only is the entire world one great big mission, but that missionary work in the spirit world is included in that same mission.

President Ezra Taft Benson said: "The spirit world is not far away. From the Lord's point of view, **it is all one great program on both sides of the veil**. Sometimes the veil between this life and the life beyond becomes very thin. This I know! Our loved ones who have passed on are not far from us" ("Because I Live, Ye Shall Live Also," *Tambuli*, Apr. 1994, 3, emphasis added). So whether we serve a mission on this side of the veil or receive the ultimate "super transfer" (i.e. we die!) and are assigned to serve in the Spirit World, it really doesn't make any difference. It isn't where we serve that will determine our ultimate reward — it is how we serve.

As you approach this wonderful time of life when the mission you had qualified to serve before the world was created approaches and you are excited about where you will serve this life-changing mission, don't forget that the details, the interviews, the formal call and assignment all precede the actual service. Make them part of your mission by doing them on time and perfectly.

*Chapter 8*

# PREPARING FOR THE
# TEMPLE ENDOWMENT

Over the years emphasis has been placed on the goal of serving a full-time mission. While that is commendable and should remain one of our goals, of greater importance is the need to prepare and enter one of the Lord's holy temples and receive the ordinances therein. While it is possible to gain the highest degree of the Celestial Kingdom without serving a full time mission, it is not possible for a person to be exalted (i.e. go the highest degree of the Celestial Kingdom) without the ordinances found only in the temple.

The wonderful part of Heavenly Father's plan is that we don't have to choose between the two goals as you would between going mountain climbing and water skiing at the same time. What the boots, ropes and climbing gear are to mountain climbing the temple is to a mission — a necessary prerequisite. It would not be possible to be successful in waterskiing without a boat, rope, skis, etc. Neither could a missionary be totally successful without the temple endowment. The temple gives one the protection against Satan and his hosts, which you will face every day of your mission. The temple endows you with knowledge and power necessary to regain the presence of God yourself and the power to help others attain the same promised condition. The temple teaches of a time when you will enter with your future mate and completes (as far as ordinance can) the final requirement necessary to return and live eternally with our Heavenly Father — temple marriage.

The temple is the most intense, comprehensive training session revealed by God for the salvation and exaltation of His children. However, to protect His children from receiving too much knowledge too soon, an all-wise Heavenly Father has placed restrictions on our entering His temples. To allow unrestricted access to the temple would be like giving an overly anxious five year old the keys to the car, with no training, and allowing him to drive. He may argue that he is prepared — adults know better. He may plead for the blessing — wise parents know he is not prepared to properly enjoy the blessing. He may accuse the parents of being discriminatory because his older brothers and sisters are allowed to drive. However, it is that very discrimination that will save his life.

Heavenly Father has a graduated course leading to exaltation in which you are in the middle. Much like finally attaining your doctor's degree, you must start with elementary school, progress through junior high school, graduate from high school, enter and complete your undergraduate degree at a university, and finally be tested for admission into graduate school. After years of study, completing assignments, tests, and writing a lengthy, difficult dissertation and defending it, you are finally qualified to receive the highest degree man can confer — the doctor's degree. So it is with the temple, there is a long and involved preparation period if you are to receive the endowment before your mission and have power in that gift.

Here is the outlined course which all of our Father's children must follow if they are to receive exaltation — also listed are the blessings associated with each step. After a person has ridden the earth around the sun a number of times (for many people in the world not privileged to be born Latter-day Saints, it is sometimes many years!), the thought occurs that there is more to life than just eating, drinking, and doing whatever feels good. As that inborn desire for something better, something higher, something more noble begins to emerge (i.e. the Spirit begins to work on them), they become receptive to the teachings of the missionaries.

Probably not in these words, but in principle they say, "Isn't there something we can do to achieve a closer relationship with our Heavenly Father?" To which question you answer, "Yes, but it will require that you sacrifice many worldly lusts and pleasures." They readily agree. So teaching takes place and at the appropriate time the ordinance of baptism is administered. Following baptism they receive the laying on of hands for the gift of the Holy Ghost. Joseph Smith taught that, "No man can receive the Holy Ghost without receiving revelations. The Holy Ghost is a revelator"(*Teachings of the Prophet Joseph Smith,* page 328).

The Holy Ghost fills the soul with joy and is the source of much learning and spiritual progress. Watch a new convert and you'll see the fire of a testimony literally transform his or her life. There is so much to learn about spiritual things and also about how temporal things fit into the kingdom of God. Immediately the new convert wants to go to the temple, but wise church leaders have restricted them for at least a year — they need time to mature, develop, and grow into the responsibilities and blessings of the temple.

Next, a male convert wants to know if there isn't more

he can do to prepare for the temple. The answer is "Yes, you can get the priesthood. But it will require even a higher standard of living and commitment than you have given as a non-priesthood-bearing member of the Church." He agrees and, after completing the interview process and agreeing to selflessly serve (a big part of priesthood responsibility), he is ordained to the priesthood. With the ordination comes the right to act in the name of God. The priesthood doesn't make him any better than anyone else, but it gives him more power and more responsibility than before he received the priesthood.

But how can he possibly know how to act like God would act? That is what the priesthood is — not only the power to act in the name of God but also the key to the revelations necessary to know how to act. There is no force associated with the priesthood. The scriptures teach a lot about the principles necessary to really be an effective priesthood leader (see D&C 121:41-45). When man acts in the name of God by the power of God, there is a thrill that non-priesthood bears never experience.

Now, being somewhat more seasoned and wanting even more association with God and Christ, the new converts ask, "Isn't there anything else we can do to gain more closeness with God?" You answer, "Yes, but in order to do so, it will require an even a higher level of commitment, more personal sacrifice, and a willingness to put away all of the evil, unclean things of the world." The convert (now having been a new member for a year or more), goes through the interview process, is given a temple recommend and then enters the temple.

Entering the temple for the first time can be overwhelming, because everything is so new. There are many false rumors circulated by Satan in his attempt to prevent a person from going to the temple. There is nothing improper, embarrassing, or uncomfortable in the temple.

Look at people you know and respect who have been through the temple. Do you really believe they would act in ways that are inappropriate? However, what you experience there will be new and different from anything you have experienced in the Church to this point. So what do you get from your willingness to strictly adhere to the high standard necessary to enter the temple? You get an endowment of knowledge and power that will enable you to enter the presence of God!

Like the preparations you make to qualify to scuba dive, so there are preparations you receive in the temple to prepare you to re-enter the presence of God. Everyone seems to be aware of the one physical, observable article associated with temple service — the garment. It is sacred, its purpose is fully explained in the temple, and it is necessary to combat the additional temptation with which Satan will surely buffet you. If you are mature (spiritually) enough to go through the temple, you are mature enough to understand the importance of wearing the garment properly for the rest of your life. If sunbathing, wearing immodest clothing, and following the fashions and trends of the world are still very important to you, perhaps you are not ready to enter the temple.

The teachings in the temple are both literal and symbolic. The literal part can be observed and understood by any person intellectual enough to correctly answer the temple recommend questions. However, the symbolic part (which constitutes the vast majority of the endowment) is wisely hidden from the unprepared by an omniscient God. There have been apostates who have lied their way into the temples and recorded the endowment session. Anyone really wanting to know what goes on in the temple could read the endowment word for word. However, it would mean absolutely nothing to them because without the Spirit and the preparation God would not reveal the deep, rich meaning behind each symbol and event.

Even though the new convert may be completely sincere in wanting to know everything contained in the endowment, it won't happen the first, tenth, or one-hundredth time they go through the temple. It will be revealed "line upon line, precept upon precept" (D&C 98:12). One manifestation of the genius of our Heavenly Father is that no unworthy or unprepared person can enter the temple and receive the deeper meaning of the endowment. They may enter the temple (the unprepared or the unworthy), but instead of being a blessing to them, it would be one of the heaviest of all cursings, because God said, "Be not deceived; God is not mocked: for whatsoever a man soweth, that shall he also reap" (Galatians 6:7).

President Ezra Taft Benson said:

I make it a practice, whenever I perform a marriage, to suggest to the young couple that they return to the temple as soon as they can and go through the temple again as husband and wife. It isn't possible for them to understand fully the meaning of the holy endowment or the sealings with one trip through the temple, but as they repeat their visits to the temple, the beauty, the significance, and the importance of it all will be emphasized upon them. (*Teachings of Ezra Taft Benson,* p.258)

Elder John A. Widstoe (an apostle some years ago) said:

To the man or woman who goes through the temple, with open eyes, heeding the symbols and the covenants, and making a steady, continuous effort to understand the full meaning, God speaks his word, and revelations come. The endowment is so richly symbolic that only a fool would attempt to describe it; it is so packed full of revelations to those who exercise their strength to seek and see, that no human words can explain or make clear the possibilities that reside in the temple service. The endowment which was given by revelation can best be understood by revelation; and to those who seek most vigorously, with pure hearts, will the revelation be greatest. ("Temple Worship," *Utah Genealogical and Historical Magazine,* April 1921, pp. 62-63)

I recall hearing President David O. McKay, I think it was at his eightieth birthday, say something like: "I am just now beginning to understand the Holy Endowment." I thought, "boy, for being a prophet you sure are slow!" Now I understand more what he was saying. It takes years, a lot of effort, and a commitment to spirituality to unlock the symbolic teachings of the temple.

After the new converts have been "endowed from on high," they are prepared to embrace the highest ordinance that God has revealed to man — eternal marriage. To this point God has not revealed a higher code of conduct expected of His children than the one required of couples who enter into the marriage covenant. In return, God promises that He will reveal to them how to become like Him.

Although I have narrated what a new convert goes through (so you'll understand when you are serving your mission), it is the same pathway you must follow in order to prepare to serve. Just for a quick review: the emptiness of life really results from the Spirit reminding the person that there is more to life than just existing. Each step in the "gospel ladder" requires greater commitment but is accompanied by greater blessings. Baptism requires you to abandon worldly ways but is rewarded by your receiving the Holy Ghost — which gives you the right to constant revelation. Priesthood requires you to get outside yourself and serve others (descriptive of what a missionary does full time) but is rewarded by God allowing you to practice using His power in a remarkable, unprecedented way. The temple endowment requires further abandonment of worldliness in dress, recreational pursuits, and characteristics but promises you the power to come into the presence of God. Finally, eternal marriage is the highest code of conduct revealed from God to man but is rewarded with the promise of being able to become like God.

Too many people enter the temple without adequate preparation and come away disappointed and unchanged. If you will prepare now for your sacred temple experience, you will not be disappointed when the day comes that you enter the temple and the level of teaching you receive is elevated from an elementary level to a doctoral level.

You can best prepare by distancing yourself now from the ways of the world. Make the necessary changes in dress, music, recreation, activities, etc. which would disqualify you or which you will have to change before you can qualify for a recommend. Look at your wardrobe (more especially you young ladies). If you cannot wear the temple garment without modifying its normal usage, then it is your wardrobe that needs to change — not the way the garment is worn. Plan now to adjust your attitude and behavior to fit the temple — not the other way around. Eliminate any course language or swearing — certainly not tolerated in the temple, which is the House of the Lord. Excessive jewelry (which includes any earrings for guys and more than one set for girls) should be eliminated. Any movies, videos, DVDs, or computer games which glorify or try to legitimize violence or sexuality should be avoided like the plague they are. You simply cannot have your membership in Zion (or the Church) and live in Babylon (or the world). People have tried unsuccessfully for years to be "worldly Saints." The end result is always the same — failure.

It really depends on how serious you are about using

the mission as a springboard for the rest of your life as to whether you start early to prepare for your sacred temple experience. The more you can study the Plan of Salvation, the purpose for life, the tactics of the adversary, the place of revelation in God's plan, how God deals with His children, and a thousand other topics you discuss every week in seminary, institute or church classes, the easier it will be for you to gain the maximum good from the temple the first time you go through.

*Chapter 9*

# NO FAREWELL BUT A GREAT START (THE MTC)

Envision in your mind's eye the loudly applauding crowd gathering to watch the Super Bowl, only to have the president of the Super Bowl organization present the winner's trophy before the game has been played. You might think the organizers have lost their ability to reason correctly, especially if they declare the event "over" and instruct the audience to return to their homes. However, somewhere back in time a tradition crept into the Church which made about as much sense as awarding the winner's trophy before the game is played. That tradition was the missionary farewell.

Friends, family, and relatives traveled for miles, many doing so at great expense, to hear a departing missionary eulogized, praised, and practically deified even before he or she had done one minute of missionary work. Some traditions are difficult to dismiss even if it is in the best interests of everyone involved. So under the signature of the First Presidency, the discontinuance of "Missionary Farewells" was announced.

Some young missionaries felt cheated — almost as

though they had been denied a "rite of passage." Really, nothing has changed. Families can still get together for socials and family pictures. Monetary gifts can still be made helping defray mission expenses. The only thing is that the sacred sacrament meeting no longer diverts the attention of the Saints from the Savior to the departing missionary. The missionary may be asked to speak on a gospel related subject — Christ-centered as it should be. The past mass migrations of young people from ward to ward following their friends at missionary farewells should be eliminated. Young men and women with many friends found that they seldom attended their own wards because they were always off to a farewell or welcome home. Seldom if ever did those attending farewells attend all three meetings. Following the sacrament meeting there would generally be an expensive open house. Seldom did the focus stay on the Savior or even keeping the Sabbath Day holy.

In their prophetic wisdom, the practice of farewells was discontinued. As we continue to respond to the direction of a living prophet, we'll see the spirituality of the people increase. So rather than mourning the passing of a tradition, let's focus on the real start of your mission.

Usually the evening before entering the MTC, the prospective missionary and his or her close family members meet with the stake president. After certifying your current worthiness, the stake president exercises his priesthood keys and sets you apart as a missionary, designates your initial assignment, and pronounces whatever blessings, cautions, and counsel he feels inspired to give. From that very moment you are a full-fledged missionary and are duty bound to obey all mission rules. You should stay with a parent or sibling of your same gender at all times, just like you are to stay with your assigned missionary companion. In other words, say your "good-byes" to boyfriends, girlfriends, and others before being set apart.

The next day, or at an assigned time, you enter the MTC. Because there are many different MTCs, you may have to fly to the designated one. Your call letter from the prophet will state where and when you are to report. Again, the practice of having large groups travel to the MTC or to the airport to "see you off" is strongly discouraged. There just isn't room to accommodate everyone who would like to see you one last time.

By the time you arrive at the MTC, your attention will likely be focused entirely on what lies ahead of you and the thoughts of having to go through emotionally painful good-byes are not all that appealing. After a very brief introduction, you are separated from your family and then the "work" in "missionary work" begins. For fifteen or sixteen hours a day you will be immersed in learning. Learning to study, learning to pray, learning to ponder, learning to discuss, learning to memorize scripture, learning the doctrine, learning to teach, learning what the Spirit feels like, learning how to answer questions, learning how to get by on less sleep than you thought possible. Learning how to learn in Heavenly Father's way and not in the ways of the world is not easy and does not come without a price. Sacrificing self is the price required.

Some experience the "spiritual bends" (like when a diver surfaces too quickly) as they come from pre-mission life, where they did very little studying, praying, or discussing. If you really want to prepare for the MTC, start now engaging family and friends in serious gospel discussions. The more you do it, the easier it becomes. If you have grown lazy and started sleeping in past 6:30 a.m., do yourself a favor and start now getting up early. The fewer major adjustments you need to make to match the MTC's daily schedule, the less likely you are to suffer the "spiritual bends." The more foreign the daily routine of the MTC from your daily schedule, the more difficulty you'll have adjusting.

Unfortunately, some newly set-apart missionaries are unwilling to make the transition to MTC life and terminate their missions before they even get started. So that you don't believe you are the only one who feels like going home, let me say that even newly called mission presidents and their wives often feel unprepared and overwhelmed at what lies ahead. So what you may misinterpret as being a revelation telling you that a mission isn't for you is really not from the Lord and is very common. Just ignore it and move ahead.

It is very likely that you'll suffer a little homesickness, even in the MTC. We will deal with homesickness in a future chapter. Here we will just raise the warning flag that feelings of homesickness are likely — don't give in to them. They will pass as you lose yourself in the work. Almost everyone will experience a bout with homesickness sometime during his or her mission. You are not alone in your feelings, but you can (as most do) overcome those feelings and move on.

Make up your mind now to stick it out during these difficult days of adjustment. You will discover, as many thousands have before you, that after the initial shock of the MTC come blessings you have never experienced before. Those blessings make all the discomfort, all the feelings of inadequacy, all the feelings of homesickness disappear like darkness when the sun comes up.

Because you have been given by the stake president the mantle of a full-time missionary, you must realize that you were set apart to represent God, Himself. Since the scriptures state: "And we have known and believed the love that God hath to us. **God is love**; and he that dwelleth in love dwelleth in God, and God in him" (1 John 4:16, emphasis added), you should know that your natural personality and appeal will be greatly increased. Even in the MTC you need to put up your defenses concerning "falling in love" with your teacher, a missionary of the opposite gender in your district, or anyone else. Because you are talking, eating, sleeping, and living the gospel 24/7 as it were, you will feel the Spirit stronger than you ever have. Unless you are aware of what is happening to you, the adversary will try to take advantage of your naivete and lure you off into romantic involvement. You are not called to find your future husband or wife in the MTC! It is just that easy. "When" (not "if") you have those strong emotional feelings, recognize them for what they are — two powerful spirits attracted to each other. You will note in the gospel that "likes attract" (see D&C 88:40). So the stronger the Spirit you have, which comes as you totally devote yourself to spiritual progress, the more likely it is that you'll have these intense feelings of love.

Don't let misinterpreted feelings of attraction ruin your foreordained mission. If you experience those feelings and feel like you are losing control of yourself, tell your branch president or your teacher. They will be able to help you overcome the temptations which will surely follow you.

Be teachable! So many young people get a little knowledge and think they have mastered the whole of the gospel. The one thing I am most sure about is that I do not know all that God has revealed. Don't get me wrong. You must learn how to question everything you have ever been taught. But there is a huge difference between questioning to doubtful disputation and questioning to understanding. If you will just phrase your questions correctly, you can have the advantage of learning why you believe what you believe. It is not only all right but expected that you will be able to document everything you know by a scripture or a quote from a latter-day prophet.

It is a lazy man's way to resort to the "hearsay gospel." The hearsay gospel goes something like "I heard that Bruce R. McConkie said one time that . . . " It requires no documentation — and very often is incorrect! Ask for a reference on everything that you haven't heard before so you have the advantage of being able to tell people which prophet said it and where they can read more about the subject.

In my classes, the very first day of class, I establish a rule. It comes as a bit of a shock until the students realize what I am saying. Because they will be me (i.e. they'll be the teacher) before long, it is imperative that they never, ever teach for doctrine their own personal belief or philosophy. So I say to them: "I really don't care what you think about the doctrine of the Church!" That really gets their attention. Then I continue: "You really don't care what I think about the doctrine of the Church. We all care what God has revealed as the doctrine of the Church!" Whenever they see me point a finger at them and then point the same finger at myself, then point that finger towards heaven, they know I'm re-emphasizing the principle: "I don't care what you think the doctrine is; you don't care what I think the doctrine is; let's discover together what the Lord has revealed as His true doctrine." Before the semester is even half over, I will get many e-mail messages from students thanking me for getting them focused on searching for God's answers to the difficult questions of life.

If I don't know the answer to a question they may ask (although I've been teaching many years and have heard almost every question young people generally ask), I will always respond by saying: "I don't know the answer to that question. I'll find an answer for you." When I find the answer, I'll report back. Only after documenting the answer will I make a definitive statement. May I invite you to follow the same example? By believing incorrect or false doctrine, we only give the adversary power to deceive people. So be teachable. If you don't know the answer, don't rest until you find it. If you can't find it, ask your teacher or your branch president. If they don't know the answer, write home or to a former seminary or institute teacher. Some questions have answers which have not been revealed. Be humble enough to accept God's wisdom in not revealing everything to His children.

Just a word of caution. Don't turn immediately to others to become your "research assistants." The real growth comes when you are willing to endure the discomfort of not knowing the answer as you continue your searching, pondering, praying, and trying to figure it out yourself. Often I'm asked how often I turn to the wall filled with gospel books and commentaries in my office to find an answer. I tell the inquiring student that in earlier years I turned to those books often. Then one day it dawned on me that those books contained the authors' insights into the very questions I was asking. I asked myself: "Why should I allow that prophet or church leader to receive the revelation that the Lord said He would give to me if I would but ask?" (see D&C 42:61). From that very day, I started searching, pondering, praying, and trying to figure it out for myself. When I come to a conclusion as to what the doctrine is, then (and only then!) would I go to the commentaries to confirm the correctness of my conclusion.

To my surprise and joy, I discovered that very often the conclusion I had reached as a result of my searching was exactly what the prophets and church leaders had written. But, having done the homework myself, those answers never left me. Whenever I answer the questions in class or on the Internet, I refer to the commentary or statement by the prophet — it seems to carry a lot more weight. But the thrill is that I know for myself, by the promised inspiration from Heaven, that what the prophets have taught is true. I found I can teach with much more power than when just reciting what they have written.

When the answer I arrive at is at odds with what the prophets have taught (which occasionally it is!), I say to myself: "I wonder where I made a mistake in my logic and reasoning?" Then I'll go back to the pondering, studying, mediating, etc. until I discover my mistake — and to this point it has **always** been "my mistake" and not the prophet's error. Be humble enough to be taught.

Sometimes a missionary will master a few scriptures and falsely believe that he or she has become a master teacher or doctrinarian. As a mission president I was amused (after the shock had passed) when a young elder was transferred to our mission from another mission for health reasons. In the initial interview he announced that he "was a master scriptorian!" I inquired as to what that meant and he informed me that he had "mastered how to locate eighty-five scriptures!" I thought if he had mastered eighty-five hundred or eighty-five thousand passages that might come closer to being a master scriptorian, but not a mere eighty-five! Be careful not to set your sights too low on how much scriptural familiarity it takes to be a true gospel scholar!

You will grow like you never have before in the MTC, but you were not called to "feed the shepherd" but to "feed the flock" (see Ezekiel 34). Once the MTC experience is over, you are to focus your entire efforts in finding and feeding the Lord's sheep. Some missionaries have a difficult time making the transition. Some want to return to the MTC, where it was so spiritually comfortable and uplifting. Everyone was on their best behavior and so highly motivated. You attended the temple every week, reinforced each other when times got tough, learned together, and felt the Spirit stronger than at any period in your life. Now the mission field is a lot tougher. It is sort of like leaving home for the first time. To learn to cook, wash clothes, clean house, and a thousand other things which you took for granted that Mom would do for you is sometimes difficult and you wanted to avoid it. However, once you make the change, you will realize that it was a necessary part of growing up and becoming independent.

You will likely look back with fondness at the MTC, as Adam and Eve must have looked back at the Garden of Eden after they were expelled. It will remain as a vision of what can be and something to strive to re-establish in the "real world" of missionary work. Glory in the experience you had and move on. The best is yet to come!!

*Chapter 10*

# PREPARE TO PRAY, WORK, LEARN, ENDURE

I remember reading the commandment to "pray always" (see Luke 18:1– and twenty other times when such commands are given in the scriptures!) and wondering what that meant. Often the command to "pray always" is followed with such phrases as: "lest ye be tempted by the devil" (3 Nephi 18:15), or "that you may come off conqueror; yea, that you may conquer Satan, and that you may escape the hands of the servants of Satan that do uphold his work" (D&C 10:5), or "that ye may not faint, until I come" (D&C 88:126) — all of which have a rather foreboding feeling. However, there are other scriptures which encourage us to "pray always" which are followed by such statements as: "that your wives and your children may be blessed" (3 Nephi 18:21), or "I will pour out my Spirit upon you, and great shall be your blessing" (D&C 19:38), or "all things shall work together for your good"(D&C 90:24).

Not only are we to "pray always" to counteract the destructive efforts of the devil, but by "praying always" we can secure the very blessings which make life not only tolerable but enjoyable. So how do we "pray always?" When I was younger and first thought about the command, I thought I should be silently talking with Heavenly Father all the time. However, I remember talking with people who would look me in the eye but were not listening to a word I was saying. It sort of irritated me. Could Heavenly Father really be asking us to look at people but basically ignore concentrating on what they were saying? I concluded that I misunderstood.

So if that is not what the command means, how are we to fulfill it? When Amulek was teaching the people to "pray always" he said: "Yea, and when you do not cry unto the Lord, let your hearts be full, drawn out in prayer unto him continually for your welfare, and also for the welfare of those who are around you" (Alma 34:27). Experience has shown that if we keep our eye focused on our eternal goal of returning to Heaven where we can live with God, then we become much more sensitive about whether a proposed activity, course of action, or behavior will take us closer to our eternal goal or become a serious detour from which we know we must sooner or later return.

Now as you talk with people (some of whom will be really rude and denigrating) you discover your reaction to them will be much more in keeping with the way Christ would handle the situation. By praying always you will soon discover that temptations lose their power. It is much easier to weigh a proposed action against the eternal cost of engaging in that action. You will see, for example, that the momentary pleasure of immorality weighed against the possible loss of serving a mission or, even broader, the possibility of losing the opportunity for eternal life, causes the "God-centered" person to shun anything that would put in jeopardy his or her chances for exaltation. One possible reason the people of the world engage in self-destructive activities is because they have no eternal perspective to balance their actions against. That is what you will take to them as a missionary!

It is not easy to "pray always" but the very success of your mission and your life depends on making this principle a working part of your everyday life. Otherwise, Satan and his followers will, almost without notice, gain power and influence over you. Be wise and learn now to "pray always."

One of the most frequently voiced frustrations of currently serving mission presidents is the lack of a good work ethic on the part of their missionaries. They complain that too many missionaries give a little effort for an hour or two and then want to quit and do "something fun." Missionary work is hard work. It requires that you be in top physical, mental, and spiritual shape. It requires that you work yourself to the point of physical exhaustion each day, get a night's sleep, get up early the next day, and do it all over again, day after day, week after week, month after month.

Those missionaries who are physically fit, eat right, get adequate rest, exercise regularly, and follow the Lord's commandment to "beware concerning yourselves" (D&C 84:43) have a much better chance of making it through their missions without serious illness. Those missionaries who fail to "give diligent heed to the words of eternal life" (ibid.) will find themselves being blindsided by the adversary and require time to recover physically, mentally, and spiritually.

If you have or want to develop a work ethic that will meet with Divine approval and not cause you to collapse while serving, start now to be "anxiously engaged in a good cause, and do many things of their own free will, and bring to pass much righteousness" (D&C 58:27). As you learn to recognize the temporal and spiritual needs of those around you, and as you listen to the promptings of the Spirit inspiring you on how to meet those needs, you will be preparing in a monumental way for missionary service. Some missionaries seem to think that they are only called to teach investigators, and if they have no investigators to teach, then they are justified in doing nothing. What a terrible mistake! You are called to identify the "elect of God" and to help meet their every need. There should never be a missionary who is bored because there isn't anything to do.

Start in your home. What could you do to lift the burden carried by your parents? Your brothers and sisters? Your neighbors and relatives? Who in the ward needs an encouraging word or a helping hand? Who in your school is outcast or needs a friend? The list is endless for those who have eyes to see. If you wait until you have been commanded, the Lord said:

> for he that is compelled in all things, the same is a slothful and not a wise servant; wherefore he receiveth no reward.... But he that doeth not anything until he is commanded, and receiveth a commandment with doubtful heart, and keepeth it with slothfulness, the same is damned. (D&C 58:26, 29)

As a mission president, I watched with disappointment as the missionaries wasted so much precious time in fruitless, self-serving ways. I spent most of my time, as I assume every mission president does, trying to motivate the missionaries to work hard every day of their missions.

Sometimes we have the mistaken idea that we have to be in school to learn. Sometimes we wait until there is a teacher assigned to teach us. Every experience in life is designed by God to be a learning experience. There seem to be two ways to learn — one is with joy and the other is with sorrow (see Jacob 4:3). You will have one of the rare opportunities of a lifetime. You will have the opportunity to observe firsthand the lives of people who are good, solid members of the church, those who are members in name only, those who are good, upright people who are not members of the church, and those who have no clue about what life is really all about. In other words, you will experience, firsthand, the broad spectrum of humanity.

You may have come from an ideal Latter-day Saint home. You may have been born and raised in a home that was anything but ideal. Or it could be anything in between. But unless you were very observant, you may not have taken the opportunity to focus on the principles which make for a successful marriage or family life. Now, with your mind enlightened by the Spirit, you are equipped to learn the lessons of godliness in a manner and at a rate you have never experienced before. Are you prepared to learn? Those who fail to learn from the mistakes of others are likely to learn with sorrow as they make the same mistakes. Also, those who fail to observe the principles which make for success in marriage and family living are likely to overlook the very keys that could make them ultimately successful in their own future marriages and family lives.

It is so easy to lose patience with those who are struggling to learn the lessons you have already learned. It is too easy to assume that everyone understands all that you know about principles which lead to happiness. It is too "missionary-like" to underestimate how many of the principles of the gospel you know which could help others overcome the marriage-threatening problems of life. Yours is the opportunity not only to learn but to teach.

Avoid comparing your current area with "the way we did it back home." There are so many more effective ways of teaching than running the risk of turning people off by "putting down" their customs and cultures. You will discover, if you don't know it already, that no one culture has a monopoly on the right way of doing things or the best of everything. Many of the marriage-enriching principles we enjoy in our marriage came from what I observed in Samoa many years ago on my first mission.

Learn to learn from the mistakes you make. You will not be a perfect missionary. You likely will not always get along with your companion. It was amusing when a frustrated missionary would call me on the phone and say: "President, I'm not here to babysit! Send my companion home! He isn't even a good member of the Church, let alone a good missionary! I am wasting my time with him!" I would try to encourage them by saying: "Now Elder, settle down. You need to learn how to get along with your companion. You'll need what you learn later in your marriage and family life." To which they would respond, "President, as long as the sun rises in the sky, I will never marry anyone remotely like my companion!" Fortunately I had much more experience than the young missionaries, so I would respond: "Elder, it is true that you can choose your mate and will never marry anyone like your companion. But it is not true that you choose your children. Unless you learn to get along with your companion, Heavenly Father will likely send one or more children to you just like your companion!" We would laugh, then I'd give them some suggestions on things they might try to improve their companionship. Not infrequently those troubled companions became some of their best mission friends.

Of course there is a limit to how long and how much you can learn from and tolerate a bad companion, but it often isn't nearly as soon as you think and you'll discover that your ability to tolerate less than an ideal relationship is much greater than you believed. Don't cut off your learning experience because of impatience. Keep your mission president informed, but follow his inspired counsel on how to continue the learning process.

You will discover early in your mission that everything takes on a different meaning when viewed under the influence of the Spirit. Without the Spirit, many of the lessons of life will escape you altogether. Strive every day of your mission to live worthy of having the Lord's Spirit as a constant companion. Be sensitive to these learning experiences. Spend more time pondering, meditating, and praying to know what lesson the Lord is trying to teach you.

You will likely realize that your prayer behavior during your growing up years left a lot to be desired. You may be very expert in praying and even in listening for answers, but never before have you been thrust into such a situation where your success was totally dependent on the Lord's help. Without Divine assistance you cannot succeed.

You will be confronted with problems, questions, situations, and frustrations, the answers to which entire escape you. Having nowhere else to turn, you'll fall to your knees and plead for Divine insight. Many times you may be in tears, believing that you've gone as far as you can go. Remember: "Man's extremity is God's opportunity" (Melvin J. Ballard, "The Inspiration of Temple Work," *Utah Genealogical and Historical Magazine*, Oct. 1932, pp 148-49). At times you'll believe that you have to get an answer "right now" because of some crisis you are facing. Keep in mind the Lord's admonition to Joseph Smith, "Therefore, let your hearts be comforted concerning Zion; for all flesh is in mine hands; be still and know that I am God" (D&C 101:16). You may substitute your name, your companion's name, a member's name, or an investigator's name for "Zion" and you'll readily see the application of this scripture.

One of the mistakes often made by members (including missionaries) is that prayer is a time when we "tell God" what we need, how to use His limitless power, or what we want Him to do and when to do it. A wise missionary or member will learn in prayer to listen more than tell. It may be uncomfortable at first, but as you persevere, the silence after you've asked a pleading question in prayer will bring some of the sweetest answers you've ever received.

Because you will be focused almost exclusively on the needs of others, you will find the remarkable truth of what the Lord said: "He that findeth his life shall lose it: and he that loseth his life for my sake shall find it" (Matthew 10:39). As you learn to "lose your life" for others, you will discover that the Lord will either remove the problems from your life or give you the wisdom and insight on how to solve them. The self-centered will never discover the truth of that great scripture. Try it and see if by focusing on the needs of others your personal problems either become manageable or disappear altogether.

One of the principles which seems to have escaped many saints is that prayer is not "ordering God around heaven" but learning to align our personal petitions with His will. If we could learn to do that perfectly, every one of our prayers would be answered (in the Lord's own due time) as we uttered them. Nephi, son of Helaman arrived at that station. Mormon records:

> Blessed art thou, Nephi, for those things which thou hast done; for I have beheld how thou hast with unwearyingness declared the word, which I have given unto thee, unto this people. And thou hast not feared them, and hast not sought thine own life, but hast sought my will, and to keep my command- ments. And now, because thou hast done this with such unwearyingness, behold, I will bless thee forever; and I will make thee mighty in word and in deed, in faith and in works; yea, even that **all things shall be done unto thee according to thy word, for thou shalt not ask that which is contrary to my will.** (Helaman 10:4-5, emphasis added)

Just one more word of caution concerning prayer: "Whatsoever ye ask the Father in my name it shall be given unto you, that is expedient for you; And if ye ask anything that is not expedient for you, it shall turn unto your condemnation" (D&C 88:64-65). Pray to know the will of God and then pray for the strength to do His will.

Finally, you must determine to endure to the end. In the vernacular of sports: "Ninety-nine yards doth not a touchdown make!" You must finish the battle to receive the prize. There may be extenuating circumstances beyond your control which would cause you to return early from your assigned mission. God knows and understands that. However, allow God — not you — to determine when "enough is enough."

There will be many times during the course of the educational opportunity called mortality when you will determine that you have reached your limit. As you plead with God to "remove this cup from me" you may discover that God is slow in eliminating your suffering. As you continue to endure, moving ahead one step at a time, you will look back from the vantage point of the future and be forced to admit that God knew you a lot better than you knew yourself.

You might think that, being on a mission, God would protect you from all suffering and danger. Some may even suggest that what you are enduring physically, mentally, and spiritually is a result of your "sinfulness." What an unhallowed thought! If suffering indicated Divine disapproval, then Christ would be the most disapproved Person ever to live! He suffered more than all of us put together. What was the result of His suffering? "Though he were a Son, yet learned he obedience by the things which he suffered; And being made perfect, he became the author of eternal salvation unto all them that obey him" (Hebrews 5:8-9).

Isn't that what is it all about? Trying to become perfect like Christ! If He became perfect by the things which He suffered, why would we be any different? You need not look for suffering and sorrow — they will find you! Don't be afraid of being tempted above what you can withstand — God won't allow it (see 1 Corinthians 10:13). If you will enter the mission field determined to be successful, then the Lord will help you accomplish your goal, because that is His goal for you.

Before you get into the thick of the battle, make your determination to be the best, most obedient, most diligent missionary ever to serve. Know you'll face opposition (as we'll discuss later), but remember you were called to succeed and not to fail.

*Chapter 11*

# WHAT IS "MY GOSPEL" YOU ARE CALLED TO TEACH?

Many years ago, I had just completed a four day MTC experience and was standing in the airport awaiting the boarding call to make the flight to Samoa — our assigned mission. There were five of us very "green" Elders. I was standing shyly off to one side when I was approached by a very professional looking woman in a business suit. Noting my discomfort in standing alone, she observed my black name tag, approached me, engaged me in conversation, and said: "Oh, I see you are a missionary. Where are you going?" I answered that I was going to Samoa. She asked, "Why are you going there?" I told her I was going to preach the gospel to the people in Samoa. She asked, "What is the gospel?" I had absolutely no idea! I must have stammered some answer that surely did not impress her but demonstrated how unprepared I was to verbalize the greatest "good news" the Lord had ever revealed. Part of my initial study of the scriptures during the early days of my full time mission was to see how the Lord defined His gospel.

Although there are many places in the scriptures where

bits and pieces of the gospel are put forth, the most comprehensive outline was given by the resurrected Savior to the Nephites. In 3 Nephi 27:13-21 the Lord defines eight points of what He terms "My Gospel." To help you avoid the same embarrassment I experienced let's outline them.

1. **Atonement** Verses 13-14:

> Behold I have given unto you *my gospel,* and **this is the gospel** which I have given unto you — that I came into the world to do the will of my Father, because my Father sent me. And my Father sent me that I might be lifted up upon the cross; and after that I had been lifted up upon the cross, that I might draw all men unto me.

The core or center of "My Gospel" is the Atonement. Without it no part of the plan of salvation would have any power or meaning. As you continue your study, you'll discover that literally everything is related to the Atonement in some way. When people accuse you of "not being a Christian," you must understand that Christ's Atonement is the hub of the wheel around which everything else revolves. There are a couple of items that are associated with this scripture that may cause you to ponder more deeply.

Why did the Savior come to work out the Atonement? He said He came "because my Father sent me." Later in this chapter (see verse 27) the Lord asks a question and then answers it Himself. "What manner of men ought ye to be? Verily I say unto you, even as I am." I often talk with Latter-day Saints who say, "I don't want to go on a mission, or accept this call, or fulfill this assignment." Yet they steadfastly declare that they are "trying to be like Jesus." If we are really trying to be like Jesus, then our desire to perform an assignment has nothing to do with our willingness to accept and complete the assignment.

The Savior's assignment was to come to earth to suffer

— to be crucified! If you knew your mission in mortality would include suffering, would you still go? Some are tested with poor health, some with accidental impairment, some with personality traits they need to overcome, and some with family problems. It doesn't appear to be the version of the test we take that really matters — it is how well we pass the test. Make up your mind now to take whatever comes to you during your mission and for the rest of your life (things over which you have no control) and make the best of it. You'll discover that discouragement almost disappears as you adopt the attitude "I'll pass this test so I can press on to eternal life."

2. **Resurrection**. Verse 14: "that as I have been lifted up by men even so should men be lifted up by the Father." The second part of "My Gospel" is put into effect because of the first — the Atonement. Without the Atonement no one would be resurrected. Jacob taught that we would become "angels to a devil" (2 Nephi 9:9) forever.

Before we can be resurrected, what has to happen? We must die! Before we can die, we must be born. Therefore, we are literally born to die! Jacob further explained, "For as death hath passed upon all men, **to fulfil the merciful plan of the great Creator**, there must needs be a power of resurrection" (2 Nephi 9:6, emphasis added). Viewed in this light, death is not some horrible monster, lurking in the shadows to rob us of our loved ones. It is part of the "merciful plan" of the Lord for the salvation and exaltation of His children. But why are we even born if we are all going to die?

3. **Judgment**. Verses 14-15:

that as I have been lifted up by men even so should men be lifted up by the Father, to stand before me, to be judged of their works, whether they be good or whether they be evil — And for this cause have I been lifted up; therefore, according to the

power of the Father I will draw all men unto me, that
they may be judged according to their works.

We are born and live to have experiences. We live so we
can one day die. We die so we can be resurrected. We are
resurrected so we can stand judgment. We are judged to
determine what kingdom of glory we have qualified to live
in for the rest of our eternal existence. Knowing that every
thought, word, and action will be weighed on the eternal
scales of justice, wouldn't it be wise to be very selective on
what we do, say, and think? Alma 12:14 states:

> For our words will condemn us, yea, all our
> works will condemn us; we shall not be found
> spotless; and our thoughts will also condemn us;
> and in this awful state we shall not dare to look up to
> our God; and we would fain be glad if we could
> command the rocks and the mountains to fall upon
> us to hide us from his presence.

The preceding verse states that he is describing only
those who harden their hearts and refuse to live by the
commandments of the gospel.

The message you take to the people of your mission is:
"Prepare for judgment by monitoring carefully what you
do, say, and think." That same message can help you
prepare, without fear, for the great judgment day. Then
you'll anticipate a "judgment unto victory" (see D&C 52:11)
and not a fearful looking forth because you have violated
the commandments of God. The next four principles of
"My Gospel" teach us how to prepare for judgment. You
will recognize them from Article of Faith number four.

4. **Faith in Jesus Christ**. Verse 19: "And no unclean
thing can enter into his kingdom; therefore nothing
entereth into his rest save it be those who have washed their
garments in my blood, because of their faith." As we
develop "faith in Christ" we see that He holds the key to our
eternal life. By learning of Him, and following Him, we

become like Him and therefore able to live eternally in His presence. Our faith motivates us to action. You may not think you have very strong faith, but the fact that you have accepted the mission call (or are preparing to) indicates that you have a powerful faith. No one gives up eighteen months or twenty-four months of their lives without having a strong, abiding faith in the cause they are teaching.

Your responsibility is to teach the Plan of Salvation with such clarity and Spirit that it creates in your investigators the desire to embrace what you are teaching. It will require practice and effort, but as you see faith begin to be planted (see Alma 32) and grow, all the sacrifices you must make to help people progress seems like a small price compared to the fruits of your labors.

5. **Repentance**. Verse 19: ". . . the repentance of all their sins." When you paint a "mind picture" so clear and so desirable to your investigators that they are willing to do whatever is necessary to achieve that goal, then the motivation to change increases, the pull of the world decreases, and changes they make in their lives to bring their behavior into line with the requirements for the Celestial Kingdom.

Unless (and until!) people see the incompatibility of their actions with the place where they want to go eternally, there is no motivation to sacrifice what the world masquerades as exciting and desirable. So your work is cut out for you — learn the gospel so well and teach it so effectively that people willingly cast off the worldly to embrace the heavenly!

Repentance, however, will only affect the way things are done in the future — that won't change past behavior. Since it is impossible to push the "reset" button and "un-sin," there must be a way to erase past mistakes.

6. **Baptism**. Verse 20: "Now this is the commandment: Repent, all ye ends of the earth, and come unto me and be baptized in my name." Baptism is the token or

manifestation that God has established as an observable action indicating the inward conviction to follow Christ. Mormon said: "Therefore, there were ordained of Nephi, men unto this ministry, that all such as should come unto them should be baptized with water, and **this as a witness and a testimony before God, and unto the people**, that they had repented and received a remission of their sins" (3 Nephi 7:25, emphasis added).

You will discover as you venture into the world that, in spite of their professed faith in Christ and His gospel, few (if any) members of other churches really understand the significance of baptism. When Adam ask the Lord why a person had to repent and be baptized (see Moses 6:53), the Lord taught Adam many wonderful and deep doctrines and then said: **"For by the water ye keep the commandment**; by the Spirit ye are justified, and by the blood ye are sanctified" (Moses 6:60, emphasis added). In other words, "You are baptized because I commanded it."

Once a person has developed faith in Christ and His "plan of happiness," has repented of his sins (i.e. determined to live according to the commandments in the future), and has been cleansed by baptism, there comes a realization that the same adversary who tripped him up previously is still alive and well. How can the new convert avoid being deceived and thus falling back into forbidden paths and becoming lost?

7. **The Gift of the Holy Ghost.** Verse 20: "that ye may be sanctified by the reception of the Holy Ghost, that ye may stand spotless before me at the last day." If a person were baptized unworthily, the blessing of forgiveness of sins would not be theirs. God's safety valve, to insure that no unworthy person receives a promised blessing, is the Holy Ghost. A person may lie to the bishop or elder interviewing him or her for baptism. That makes no difference, because it is impossible to lie to God.

The Holy Ghost acts as a Guide to help us detect and avoid the pitfalls placed in our pathway by the devil and his angels. Without that Divine help we are destined to stumble and fall frequently. Remember: "The Holy Ghost is a revelator. No man can have the Holy Ghost without receiving revelation" (*Teachings of the Prophet Joseph Smith*, page 328).

The Holy Ghost will not only lead you away from the spiritual traps of Satan but will inspire or prompt you regarding whom to visit, what to teach them, how to answer their questions, and then will bear witness to the truthfulness of what you are teaching (see 2 Nephi 33:1). With the help of the Holy Ghost, you cannot fail; without it, you cannot succeed.

The Holy Ghost is the Divine influence that "fills your soul with joy" (see D&C 11:13-14) and teaches you everything you need to know to be a successful missionary and a successful person when your full time mission is completed. Books have been written (and more need to be!) about the influence of the Holy Ghost in our lives.

8. **Endure to the end.** Verse 16: "If he endureth to the end, behold, him will I hold guiltless before my Father at that day when I shall stand to judge the world." What a sad thing to see a fired-up young missionary return, testify of the value of the mission, and then fall away into forbidden paths. It doesn't need to happen. But when one goes from doing Christlike service all day every day to being totally consumed in personal gratification, it doesn't take long to strangle the Spirit. Once the Spirit withdraws, it is just a matter of time before spiritual malnutrition takes its toll and the person finds his name on the rolls of the less-than-active.

Some erroneously believe that their past missionary experience has earned them a seat in the Celestial Kingdom. Ezekiel saw people like that and wrote:

But when the righteous turneth away from his righteousness, and committeth iniquity, and doeth according to all the abominations that the wicked man doeth, shall he live? All his righteousness that he hath done shall not be mentioned: in his trespass that he hath trespassed, and in his sin that he hath sinned, in them shall he die. (Ezekiel 18:24)

The key is to keep growing, serving, and progressing.

"Enduring to the end" sometimes has a negative connotation. It shouldn't! It really means that what you started to evolve into as a new convert (whether you were born into the Church or converted later on), you continued to improve as a missionary, and will continue to progress until you have fulfilled what the Lord said in answer to His own question: "What manner of men ought ye to be? Verily I say unto you, even as I am!" (3 Nephi 27:27).

Enduring to the end isn't difficult — you do it just one day at a time. One cannot envision a God who is righteous one day and then wicked the next — alternating whenever He desires. God is God because of His consistency. If we are going to be like Him, we must develop the same steadiness He has and then practice it until we die.

Now there are the eight points of "My Gospel" — 1. Atonement; 2. Resurrection; 3. Judgment; 4. Faith in Christ; 5. Repentance; 6. Baptism; 7. The Gift of the Holy Ghost; and 8. Enduring to the end. If you are wise, you will take whatever time is necessary to prepare a talk on the overview of the eight points outlined in the Gospel and then a talk on each of the eight points. You will have nine well prepared, scripturally documented, logically presented talks so that when (not if) the bishop or branch president sees you and your companion walk into sacrament meeting, approaches you, and asks you to be today's sacrament meeting speakers, you will be fully prepared and without fear.

When our missionaries were approached by the bishop or branch president (which happened frequently), they asked what he wanted them to talk on. He would, with relief in his voice, say, "Oh, just talk about the gospel." Automatically nine topics came to mind! You can do the same.

Over the years of using the example of me standing in the airport not knowing what the gospel was, I have received numerous letters and e-mail messages from missionaries serving in various places around the world. Many have confessed that when approached by inquiring people and asked about what they were doing and where they were going, that they could hardly wait to explain the "Eight Points of My Gospel."

One sister missionary wrote that when a man asked her the question "what is the gospel?"she listed off the eight points. She said that his more than obvious first intention was not to learn about the Church but to make a romantic pass at her. As she explained the points of "My Gospel" his whole attitude changed. He gave her his business card and asked if she would send his name in as a referral. She reported that several months later she received a letter from him stating that he had been baptized and was now preparing to serve a mission. He confessed his original intent to flirt with her, apologized and asked her forgiveness. He attributed his interest to her ability to verbalize the principles of the gospel and the Spirit he felt as she bore her testimony.

Hopefully when you are confronted from now on, you'll be able to do what so few can do with power and conviction — explain what the gospel you are called to teach is.

*Chapter 12*

# MAKING A RECORD OF
# YOUR MISSION

In my book *Serve With Honor*, I explained in some detail about keeping three records of your mission: 1. Letters home; 2. personal journal; and 3. weekly letters to your mission president. I will not go into the same detail in this chapter but want to add some thoughts that may enrich your mission record and enable you to use those records in teaching your children and grandchildren for generations to come.

There seems to be a "fact of life" that is often overlooked when a person is young — that you will always remember the significant things that happen to you. I had been serving as an assistant to the mission president for a number of months when my companion and I organized and executed a week-long mission conference in a place President David O. McKay said he thought was the most beautiful spot on earth — Sauniatu, Samoa. It is situated in the top of an extinct volcano and is breathtakingly beautiful. The conference had been well planned and everything unfolded exactly as planned.

During the course of the week something happened

that really impressed me. I recorded in my journal: "I have just had one of the most transcendent spiritual experiences of my life. One that I shall never forget!" That was the sum of my entry. Now many years later I have tried to recall what the "spiritual experience" was — it is gone! If you want to remember something, write it down. Memories fade, details are forgotten, and teaching opportunities are forfeited if you fail to take time to record what you are experiencing.

Often Satan tries to use our lack of progress as a manifestation that we really aren't getting anywhere! That is why he is called "a liar from the beginning" (see D&C 93:25). To counteract that false impression of non-progress, why not write yourself a letter the day you leave the MTC? Explain what you think a mission will be like, bear your testimony to yourself, sign your letter, put your name on the envelope and put it aside until the end of your mission. Sister Bott gave the incoming missionaries some blue stationary to write on as part of our entrance process. I would then place their sealed envelopes in a folder along with their weekly mission president's letters. During their exit interview, I would present them the president's letters and the sealed envelope they had written the day they arrived in the mission field.

Often I would hear boisterous laughter from the waiting room where the outgoing missionaries were waiting for their exit interview. When questioned about the cause of the outburst, they would often read me portions of the letters they had written to themselves. Many hadn't realized the tremendous lessons they had learned while serving their missions. Some had thought they were so mature and seasoned only to discover that they were young and naive. You might consider writing yourself a letter now and then reading it later when you really need a "pick-me-up." The progress you will make, because you live with yourself all the time and experiences and progress seem so small and slow, may not be as noticeable as when you look back from a future vantage point upon the accumulated progress. Then you'll be amazed at how much you've changed. High school reunions tend to have the same affect when you attend after having served a mission. The difference between those who serve and those who chose not to is so remarkable you wouldn't believe it unless you witnessed it first hand.

You will find as you teach and study the gospel that little flashes of inspiration will come. Often they happen as you are trying to fashion an answer to a difficult question or in giving counsel to someone in need. They are usually "one-liners." Turn to the very last page in your missionary journal and at the top of the page write "Inspiration I have received!" Then every time you get one of these spiritual flashes, jot it down in the back of your journal. Before long you'll see that the insights become almost like a personal compilation of revelations or insights given directly to you by a loving Heavenly Father. Much of what I teach in the Missionary Preparation classes at BYU comes from insights I received as a mission president.

It is a sad day when a missionary discovers, too late, that he or she should have taken time to record not only "what" happened during the endless days of the mission, but also "how they felt" about what they experienced. You may even remember "what" you experienced, but after about a week the "how you felt" will begin to dissipate. Then you will be left with a rather sterile accounting or travelogue of what you did day by day. As one who looks back with some regret at not having been more diligent as a young missionary, let me warn you to avoid the mistake I made.

I became so busy doing that I forgot to record. As the years march on, I am left to wonder whether certain things really happened or whether my romantic imagination has been working overtime. Thankfully I have just enough detail recorded to know that many of the miraculous things that I remember really did happen. I just wish I had more names and a lot more detail included in my journal entries.

The "white bible" (Missionary Handbook) mandates that you "write to your parents each week on preparation day" and that you "limit other correspondence" (see page 21 of the Missionary Handbook). Remember, without being totally obedient, you cannot enjoy the fulness of the Spirit. So even if you are not that thrilled at taking time to write a weekly letter to your parents, do it anyway! The level of success you will enjoy as a missionary depends on the level of obedience you exhibit to the commandments and the mission rules.

Share your mission with your family. You don't need to "preach" to them or "call them to repentance" — that isn't your stewardship. However, you can and should share with them the lessons you are learning and the impact the gospel is having on your own and your investigators' lives. You can and should encourage your family in the challenges they are facing and express your love to them often. Let the Spirit do the rest.

After a rather lengthy separation from their families, Joseph Smith and Sidney Rigdon were concerned about their welfare. The Lord revealed: "Verily, thus saith the Lord unto you, my friends Sidney and Joseph, your families are well; they are in mine hands, and I will do with them as seemeth me good; for in me there is all power. Therefore, follow me, and listen to the counsel which I shall give unto you" (D&C 100:1-2). Since you have neither all knowledge or all power, it seems wise to leave your family in the hands of the Lord and go about your assigned duties. Occasionally things happen at home which tempt you to terminate (or at least interrupt) your mission to go home and help stabilize things there. Put the thought out of your mind and let the Lord bless your family because of your service. He revealed: "Therefore, thrust in your sickle with all your soul, and your sins are forgiven you, and you shall be laden with sheaves upon your back, for the laborer is worthy of his hire. Wherefore, your family shall live" (D&C 31:5). Remember: "I the Lord am bound when ye do what I say!" (D&C 82:10).

Even if you have a poor relationship with one or both of your parents, write to them and allow the Lord to work on them through your letters. A young elder from Ireland had a father who was not a member of the church and was very opposed to his son serving a mission. This elder was already serving when we arrived to begin our mission. He explained that he really didn't want to write to his father because the return letters were filled with poison, accusations, condescending remarks, and put-downs. I promised him that if he would write weekly that the Lord would soften his father's heart before the elder completed his mission. With a twinkle in his Irish eye he said, "Even the Almighty cannot soften the heart of an Irishman!" I told him to give God a chance. I told him to be positive, loving, and non-condemning and leave the rest up to the Lord.

Month after month no apparent progress was made from the home front. His father was even more negative as he responded to his missionary son's letters. Finally, as I drove back to the mission home following the next to last zone conference for this Elder, I was complaining to the Lord. I prayed, "Heavenly Father, I thought I felt impressed to promise this elder that You would soften his father's heart. He goes home next month and no apparent progress has been made. I'm afraid he'll go home disillusioned at the promise his mission president made many months ago. Isn't that angel You sent to straighten Alma the Younger and the Sons of Mosiah still available?"

At the next zone conference this faithful elder came

running to me exclaiming "I got it! I got it! President, it was just like you promised! I got it!" I calmed him down and he thrust a letter into my hands. It was from his father. In part it said, "Son, I have been nothing but negative and condescending to you for the full two years you have served in California. You have done nothing but write back your love for me and told how this gospel has changed your own and the lives of those you are teaching. I can't promise I will join your church, but the Sunday you get home, I want to go to church with you and I want you to teach me those six missionary discussions." Miracles happen when we are obedient to the Lord and His gospel.

By conscientiously writing home every week — not just a travelogue but real experiences, punctuated by the Spirit, you will have an unparalleled record of the inspiring, upbeat experiences of your mission. You will have a documented record of your growth spiritually and in your understanding of the doctrines of the gospel. You will have a record of how you met and overcame obstacles common to all missions and those which are peculiar to your mission.

I would suspect (even without you suggesting it) that your parents will keep all of your letters for future reference. If you think they might not, you might suggest they get a shoe box and keep them for future reference. Before many years have passed, you'll see the absolute value of the letters you've written just as we read, with great interest, the letters Paul, the Apostle, wrote to the people in the different branches of the Church in his day. You may be writing scripture for your future family — write well and thoughtfully.

Often if a missionary has a special someone waiting for him or her, he or she wants to write about them in their journals. Caution should be exercised since only about one in every ten actually waits for the missionary. Therefore, you likely are writing about someone else's future husband or wife. To avoid embarrassment, I would suggest you keep personal feelings about a girlfriend or boyfriend to a minimum — and if you are learning a new language, you may decide to write everything of a personal nature in your foreign language! It could save future embarrassment.

I had five girls waiting for me when I left (I erroneously thought there was "security in numbers" — wrong). They all five ended up marrying other men while I was serving. But one of my "one-liners at the end of my journal" is "Remember: your boyfriend or girlfriend may marry someone else while you are serving, your husband or wife will not!" Thankfully I wrote all I did about my girlfriends in Samoan. When my children would ask what the Samoan in my journal said, I would respond by saying: "That is just a reminder to me not to be stupid!" They would respond, "Dad, you sure had to remind yourself not to be stupid a lot!" That was far superior than trying to explain what I had romanticized as an immature missionary.

A final record would be those weekly letters written to your mission president, who acts as the Savior's representative to you. I always encouraged our missionaries to write as though they were reporting their weekly activities to the Savior. Those who took the time and thoughtfully wrote had a rich record of the frustrations they were having, the hopes and dreams they were experiencing, and the plans they were making on how to defeat the adversary in their areas.

Unfortunately, a number of missionaries did not take seriously the challenge. Such was one Elder Allen. Encourage him as I would, he would not consistently write his president's letters. When he did, it was something like: "Hi Prez. Hope all is going well. I'm cool. Write to you next week." Nothing of substance. On the day of his exit interview, as I returned his mission president's letters to him, he looked at the nearly empty folder containing only a dozen or so letters, none of which were worth reading, and realized that he had really robbed himself of a meaningful record of his mission. While other elders were leafing through the 104 letters they had written and the sisters through the almost 80 letters they had written, he had only a dozen scraps of paper with nonsense scribbled on them. There wasn't anything I could do or say at that time. I had tried to warn him many times that the day would come when he would regret not writing. He would say: "I know, I know. You're doing your job Prez. I'll tell the GAs that you've done your thing!" It wasn't until that final day that he realized that I had "done my thing" but that he hadn't. I have seldom seen such regret in a missionary's eyes as I did that day with Elder Allen. Don't make the same mistake. Write diligently, write thoughtfully, write passionately, and then when you get your president's letters back, you'll have yet another wonderful record of your mission from which to teach family and Church members for the rest of your life.

## Chapter 13

# EXPECTING OPPOSITION, USING SATAN AGAINST SATAN

You have probably heard before that you will experience satanic opposition in the mission field. You might even mistakenly believe that everyone on earth receives the same devilish attention as they try to do good. The Lord revealed two passages of scripture which will help you understand the unique nature of the temptations you will be facing. "And it must needs be that the devil should tempt the children of men, or they could not be agents unto themselves; for if they never should have bitter they could not know the sweet" (D&C 29:39). Understandably, the devil "should tempt" the people of the world in order to provide a contrast between good and evil. However, in describing Satan's reaction to the chosen Saints, the Lord revealed, "Wherefore, he maketh war with the saints of God, and encompasseth them round about" (D&C 76:29). Can you see the difference in intensity between "tempt" and "maketh war with"?

For you to mistakenly believe that you are just another person for Satan to tempt would be playing into his hands. Brigham Young taught: "The men and women, who desire to obtain seats in the celestial kingdom, will find that they must battle with the enemy of all righteousness every day" (*Journal of Discourses*, 11:14).

Many young people really become serious about living a more Christlike life as they begin to prepare for their missions. At the very moment of your decision to serve, you can expect satanic opposition. You will recall that just before the First Vision, when the Father and the Son appeared to Joseph Smith, he had a terrible fight with the adversary. He thought he was going to be destroyed, so powerful was the opposition. It was only with the appearance of the "pillar of light" that he was liberated from this destructive influence.

You may remember how Moses (see Moses 1) stood in the presence of God and saw the majesty of His creations. When God withdrew from Moses, Satan appeared and tempted him. It is a true gospel principle that will benefit you all your life if you realize that "God never gives a superior blessings without an equal and opposition temptation." Brigham Young forcefully taught:

> I ask, is there a reason for men and women being exposed more constantly and more power-fully to the power of the enemy, by having visions than by not having them? There is and it is simply this — God never bestows upon His people, or upon an individual, superior blessings without a severe trial to prove them, to prove that individual, or that people to see whether they will keep their covenants with him, and keep in remembrance what He has shown them. Then the greater the vision, the greater the display of the power of the enemy. And when such individuals are off their guard they are left to themselves, as Jesus was. For this express purpose the Father withdrew His Spirit from His Son, at the time he was to be

crucified. Jesus had been with his Father, talked with Him, dwelt in His bosom, and knew all about heaven, about making the earth, about the transgression of man, and what would redeem the people, and that he was the character who was to redeem the sons of earth, and the earth itself from all sin that had come upon it. The light, knowledge, power, and glory with which he was clothed were far about, or exceeded that of all others who had been upon the earth after the fall, consequently at the very moment, at the hour when the crisis came for him to offer up his life, the Father withdrew Himself, withdrew His Spirit, and cast a vail over him. That is what made him sweat blood; but all was withdrawn from him, and a veil was cast over him, and he then plead with the Father not to forsake him. "No," says the Father, "You must have your trials, as well as others."

So when individuals are blessed with visions, revelations, or great manifestations, look out, then the devil is nigh you, and you will be tempted in proportion to the vision, revelation, or manifestation you have received. Hence thousands, when they are off their guard, give way to the severe temptations which come upon them, and behold they are gone. (*Journal of Discourses* 3:205-206)

Translated into our daily lives, then, we should expect increased temptations either just before or just after we receive our mission calls, just before or just after going through the temple; just before or just after being set apart, just before or just after arriving at the Missionary Training Center. The "equal and opposites" will continue after your mission as you get engaged, get married, have children, receive callings in the Church, etc. If you know what is happening, you can almost gauge how well you are doing by the amount of opposition you are receiving.

If you are wise and have had a "pillar of light" experience, then you'd better redouble your defensive efforts against Satan in preparation for the "equal and opposite." Also, if you are being kicked around by the adversary and haven't had a spiritual experience, then hang on (as Joseph Smith did), and soon you'll enjoy an "equal and opposite" on the good side. What a valuable key in recognizing and controlling the "enemy of all righteousness."

It seems like we are at a disadvantage when we consider that Satan and his followers have had thousands of years of experience at tempting billions of people. Additionally, he doesn't seem to have a veil between him and our pre-earth life — we do, he doesn't. So how can we expect to win when engaged in battle with him? We'll talk more of that in the next chapter, but for right now, let's consider several techniques to give us the upper hand in the battle against evil. First, remember that "All beings who have bodies have power over those who have not. The devil has no power over us only as we permit him. The moment we revolt at anything which comes from God, the devil takes power" (*Teachings of the Prophet Joseph Smith* p.181). So our bodies not only become instruments that Satan uses to tempt us, but they also are the very tools which gives us power over Satan and his followers. It depends on whether we control our bodies or our bodies control us.

Too often people get the mistaken impression that we are helpless victims when fighting Satan. Not so! It is true that once bad habits are ingrained they may be difficult to change, but change them we can! Perhaps an example will clarify this principle: One day I received a telephone call from a distraught Elder who said he had committed the "unpardonable sin" and needed to be sent home. I asked him if he had murdered someone against light and knowledge? He said "no" and requested that I not joke with him. I told him it was no joke because the Lord defined the "unpardonable sin" in Doctrine and Covenants 132:27. He didn't live too far from the mission office so I drove to his apartment to find him packing his bags in preparation for his departure. His trainee was beside himself not knowing what was wrong or what to do. I excused the "greeny" and talked with the weeping elder. He said that things had been going very well, families had accepted the challenge to be baptized, and the ward members were really getting behind the missionaries. He lamented that in a state of exhaustion he had gone to bed only to awaken having masturbated. He was sure that was the "unpardonable sin" for a missionary. If he hadn't been so intense, I would have been tempted to laugh.

I assured him that self-abuse, although wrong and undesirable, was not the unpardonable sin and that he wouldn't have to be sent home. We could work out the problem while he served. He was comforted and his trainee was very relieved. I suggested that the elder put the past behind him, focus on serving an honorable mission and move ahead. He agreed.

Two weeks later he called and said he had slipped again. I drove to his apartment and asked what he had been thinking about? He said that he had been concentrating 24/7 on not doing it. I thought that sounded alright to me so I told him I would take it up with the Lord and see what inspiration I could get. I resorted to a park where I usually went when I needed some Divine insight. As I laid out the problem to the Lord it was as if someone lifted the top of my head and poured in a quart of inspiration. The words were clear and all but audible. It was like someone was saying: "Dear President Bott, don't you realize that if the adversary can get a person to either think about 'doing it' or think about 'not doing it', they are still thinking about 'it!'

Knowing a little of how the devil works, if he can get you to focus on the 'forbidden fruit' long enough — either with the thought of 'doing it' or 'not doing it', he can weaken you until you finally give in."

That seemed so obvious that I wondered why I hadn't connected the dots before. Now the course of action to be taken was rather obvious. Every time you catch yourself thinking about doing something wrong or thinking about not doing something wrong you need to stop immediately and use that thought of sin as a catalyst to remind you to do something you know you ought to be doing. For instance, if you discover your attention is focused on something undesirable (either to do or to think about not doing), you immediate say: "Thank you Satan for reminding me to...." then have a Plan A-E of things you want to do that are positive. For example, Plan A might be to read a chapter in the Book of Mormon; Plan B — memorize a passage of scripture; Plan C — offer a prayer of thanks for the Atonement; Plan D — sing an inspirational song; or Plan E — do an act of service. You could have as many plans as necessary.

Although Satan is not intelligent, he is not stupid either. When he sees that you are not falling for his deceptive tricks, then he'll back off. Will he leave you entirely alone? Not likely. But he may try to hit you from a different direction — which is often easier to resist.

Take a pro-active approach to overcoming Satan's influence. In Samoa where I served many years ago, many of the women would only dress from the waist down. It was really distracting to a Utah farm boy. So, knowing that the temptation to look below the nose would always be there, we decided that we would write passages of scriptures on three by five cards and when the temptation came we would say: "Thanks, Satan, for reminding me to memorize another passage of scripture." Then we'd pull a card from our pockets and memorize a scripture. Over the two and a half years I served in Samoa I mastered hundreds of scriptures since the opportunities to "look below the nose" were almost constant.

I have adopted the phrase "Using Satan against Satan" to describe that process of using Satan's temptations as a catalyst to remind me to do something I want to do. Could that technique help you overcome whatever you are struggling to master? If the "plans" I have outlined don't work for you, devise some that do! The main thing is that you realize that you can (with the help of the Savior) overcome all the temptations the devil can throw in your pathway.

Rather than making perfecting yourself such a drudgery, why not make a game of it? Select the one characteristic, habit, or trait you know you must overcome before you will be welcome in the Celestial Kingdom. It might be swearing, lusting, anger, sarcasm, gossip, or any of a hundred other traits the devil has succeeded in infiltrating into your character. Now consciously work on the biggest "Goliath" or weakness you have to overcome. You may discover that the habit is so deeply ingrained in your personality that it takes some time to overcome. You hit your "Goliath" with everything you've got. Likely he'll hit you back and even knock you down. Don't be discouraged. Get back up and try again. After some time you'll start to get the upper hand. Before long your Goliath will be on the ropes. If you persist you'll find you've overcome the problem you thought you would never be able to conquer. Now, emboldened by your success, you find a couple more smaller habits or Goliaths which were lurking behind the big one you just destroyed. You tackle them the same way. Just consciously identify and systematically work to overcome them.

Before long, you'll have knocked down two and be

ready to tackle the five or six smaller faults behind the Goliaths you just dispatched. Now perfecting yourself has become a game. It is so much fun to become aware of habits you need to break you can hardly wait for the next challenge. It gives you a sense of the power in controlling the adversary. There isn't anything you can't accomplish with the help of the Lord. The Savior revealed: "For verily I say unto you, I will that ye should overcome the world; wherefore I will have compassion upon you" (D&C 64:2).

One of the helps which Heavenly Father has offered to you to assist in your overcoming of weaknesses is spiritual gifts. President George Q. Cannon said:

How many of you are seeking for these gifts that God has promised to bestow? How many of you, when you bow before your Heavenly Father in your family circle or in your secret places, contend for these gifts to be bestowed upon you? How many of you ask the Father in the name of Jesus to manifest Himself to you through these powers and these gifts? Or do you go along day by day like a door turning on its hinges, without having any feeling upon the subject, without exercising any faith whatever, content to be baptized and be members of the Church and to rest there, thinking that your salvation is secure because you have done this? [...] If any of us are imperfect, it is our duty to pray for the gift that will make us perfect. Have I imperfections? I am full of them. What is my duty? To pray to God to give me the gifts that will correct these imperfections.[...] They are intended for this purpose. No man ought to say, "Oh, I cannot help this; it is my nature." He is not justified in it, for the reason that God has promised to give strength to correct these things and to give gifts that will eradicate them.[...] That is the design of God concerning His children. He wants His Saints to be perfected in the truth. (*Gospel Truth*, Vol. 1, p.195-196)

Rather than becoming discouraged at how many weaknesses you have and how far you have to go to reach perfection, why not start where you are at and build from there? In the oft-quoted scripture in Ether 12:27, the Savior promises that He will make weak things become strong to you, if you will just humble yourself and seek His help.

Will the satanic opposition ever cease? Yes, there are two ways. First is to die! If you are righteous at the time of death, Satan will cease to have power over you. Second, sin! If you sin to the point that you disqualify yourself from fulfilling your foreordained mission, the temptations will likely subside because you no longer pose a threat to Satan and his kingdom. But as long as you are fighting the true Christian warfare, you can expect opposition. President Ezra Taft Benson taught:

For nearly six thousand years, God has held you in reserve to make your appearance in the final days before the Second Coming of the Lord.[...] While our generation will be comparable in wickedness to the days of Noah, when the Lord cleansed the earth by flood, there is a major difference this time. It is that God has saved for the final inning some of his strongest children, who will help bear off the Kingdom triumphantly. And that is where you come in, for you are the generation that must be prepared to meet your God.

All through the ages the prophets have looked down through the corridors of time to our day. Billions of the deceased and those yet to be born have their eyes on us. Make no mistake about it — you are a marked generation. There has never been more expected of the faithful in such a short period of time as there is of us. Never before on the face of this earth have the forces of evil and the forces of good been as well organized. Now is the great day of the devil's power, with the greatest mass murders of all time living among us. But now is also the great day of the Lord's power, with the greatest number ever of priesthood holders on the earth. And the showdown is fast approaching. ( "In His Steps," in *Speeches of the Year,* 1979 Provo: BYU Press, 1980, page 59)

So, welcome to the battle of all battles. Congratulations on being found worthy to join the ranks of the Savior's elite guard. It will be a battle the likes of which you have never fought before. But the outcome is sure. The only thing in question is where you will stand when the battle is over. Prepare now for the weighty responsibility which will soon fall on your shoulders.

*Chapter 14*

# YOUR KEY TO SURVIVAL –
# PUTTING ON THE WHOLE
# ARMOR OF GOD

It is true that we live in very tough times. How tough? Sufficiently tough that unless you understand who you are and what you represent, the likelihood of your surviving the last days preceding the Second Coming is not good. Even if you know who you are, unless you follow the prescribed way to survive, your chances for physical and spiritual survival are only dim hopes. So this chapter becomes more than just something nice to talk about, it becomes your key to survival.

Thousands of years ago Enoch and his city were in the process of being taken off the earth. The whole earth had become corrupted and so evil that Enoch's city — called Zion, could no longer exist in such a wicked environment. Enoch was standing along side the pre-mortal Christ, viewing the history of the earth as it would unfold. Then Enoch saw a blood-chilling vision: "And he beheld Satan; and he had a great chain in his hand, and it veiled the whole face of the earth with darkness; and he looked up and laughed, and his angels rejoiced" (Moses 7:26). Enoch looked to the Savior for assurance that everything was alright and noticed the Savior weeping. Having the whole of eternity spread before him, Enoch was confused why the Savior would weep over such a small, insignificant earth as this one. He stated that if the man could number the particles of sand necessary to make up this earth and millions of earths just like it, it would only be a beginning to the number of earths the Savior had created, and he couldn't begin to see the end of His creations. The Savior agreed with Enoch's observation concerning the magnitude of His creation and acknowledged that He knew what was going on with the people on each of those earths (see Moses 7:27-35) and then put our earth into eternal perspective. "Wherefore, I can stretch forth mine hands and hold all the creations which I have made; and mine eye can pierce them also, and among all the workmanship of mine hands there has not been so great wickedness as among thy brethren" (Moses 7:36). Think of it! The most wicked earth ever peopled by the children of our Heavenly Father, and you were assigned to live here!

In a way that makes you very special. Why? Because Heavenly Father would not send spirit sons and daughters here unless He knew we could counteract the tremendous evil that would surround us. Taking it one step further– on this most wicked earth, there are four times that have been identified as more wicked than the rest. The first was during the days of Noah when the "earth was filled with violence" (Genesis 6:11) and the "thoughts of their hearts were only evil continually" (Moses 8:22). It seems the only thing they ever thought of was violence and sexual perversions! Aren't you glad we don't live during those days? The Lord cleansed the earth of all living things, preserving only Noah and his family and a representation of the animals and birds.

The second time listed as the most wicked on this most wicked world was during the days when Christ lived on the earth. Nephi recorded:

Wherefore, as I said unto you, it must needs be expedient that Christ—for in the last night the angel spake unto me that this should be his name — should come among the Jews, among those who are the more wicked part of the world; and they shall crucify him — for thus it behooveth our God, and there is none other nation on earth that would crucify their God.

For should the mighty miracles be wrought among other nations they would repent, and know that he be their God. (2 Nephi 10:3-4)

The third time mentioned in scriptures and by living prophets as being the most wicked is the days in which you live—just preceding the Second Coming. It is described "as it was in the days of Noah, so shall it be in the days of the Coming of the Son of Man" (Joseph Smith Matthew 1:41). The Prophet Joseph Smith, President Joseph Fielding Smith, and others (see Bruce R. McConkie, *The Millennial Messiah*, p.45) taught that our generation was as wicked as the one who crucified Christ and if He were to come again, we would attempt to crucify Him again. "This generation is as corrupt as the generation of the Jews that crucified Christ; and if He were here today, and should preach the same doctrine He did then, they would put Him to death" (*Teachings of the Prophet Joseph Smith*, p.328).

In essence the Lord revealed that our day is like a combination of Noah's day and the Savior's day. The only time that could be worse would be during the little season at the end of the millennium when "the thousand years are ended, and men again begin to deny their God, then will I spare the earth but for a little season; And the end shall come, and the heaven and the earth shall be consumed and pass away, and there shall be a new heaven and a new earth" (D&C 29:22-23). I have included the references so you would have them as you teach the doctrine to others.

So how can one possibly stand during these troubled, evil times? The Apostle Paul and the Prophet Joseph Smith both gave the inspired key: Put on the whole armor of God! In Ephesians 6:11-17 and Doctrine and Covenants 27:15-18 the Lord gives a warning and the solution. The comparisons I will make originally came to my attention through the teachings of President Harold B. Lee (see *Stand Ye In Holy Places* in the chapter entitled "Your coat of armor"), the analogies are my own.

> Put on the whole armour of God, that ye may be able to stand against the wiles of the devil. For we wrestle not against flesh and blood, but against principalities, against powers, against the rulers of the darkness of this world, against spiritual wickedness in high places.

> Wherefore take unto you the whole armour of God, that ye may be able to withstand in the evil day, and having done all, to stand. (Ephesians 6:11-13)

It might be easier if we had an enemy who was like us — flesh and blood — but we don't. We are faced with a foe who is not visible to the human eye — the devil. Paul lays out the case directly: put on the armor of God in the evil day before the Second Coming and you will stand. Fail to put it on and you will not stand! You can see the imperative nature of coming to a functional understanding of how to put on this invisible armor.

Starting with the area of the body which he knew would come under the greatest attack, Paul instructs: "Stand therefore, having your loins girt about with truth" (verse 14). According to President Lee, the loins represent our virtue. He declares that the only thing that will protect our virtue during these last days is "truth." If we fail to make application of the "truth", then it will do no more to protect us than if we didn't understand at all.

Doctrine and Covenants 93:24 states that "truth is knowledge of things as they are, and as they were, and as they are to come." Said another way, truth could be defined as the way things are here in mortality, as they were during our pre-mortal existence, and as they will be during the endless duration of eternity. So the truth that protects our virtue during times when immorality is paraded as acceptable and "everybody is doing it" is: "abuse it now and run the risk of losing the power to procreate forever!" That is the truth! Allow the temporarily borrowed procreative powers to control you (use them without Divine permission), and you run the risk of not having them restored to your resurrected body. Only those in the highest degree of the Celestial Kingdom will have the power to procreate (see D&C 131:1-4), all else will live "separately and singly in their saved condition" (see D&C 132:15-17). So the choice is yours — will you trade a momentary thrill for the opportunity to live together as families for the rest of your eternal life? Given that choice, a wise young person will always choose to remain chaste.

One more truth that may help you maintain your virtue as well as determine what is and is not appropriate on a date would be the following exercise: consider that your future husband or wife (whom you have not yet met) is on a date with another person. Think about the steps of physical intimacy beginning with holding hands and progressing all the way through sexual intercourse. When you get to the point that you don't want another person doing that particular activity with your future mate, then you have defined the degree of sexual involvement you can be involved in on your dates. It is total hypocrisy to expect a higher degree of chastity from your future mate than you require of yourself. Think that one over and make whatever adjustments are necessary to keep your loin covering of truth firmly in place.

Next, "having on the breastplate of righteousness" (Ephesians 6:14). The breastplate according to President Lee covers your vital organs as typified by your heart. He compares your heart to your conduct. What protects your conduct? Righteousness! Again we must look for a definition and application or our conduct will not escape the deceptive darts of the adversary.

What is "righteousness?" What is "right?" What God says is right is right and what God says is wrong is wrong! If you want to argue with that definition, you will never stand in the evil day. Isaiah saw that people in our day would "call evil good, and good evil; that put darkness for light, and light for darkness; that put bitter for sweet, and sweet for bitter!" (Isaiah 5:20).

The Lord has graciously provided living prophets, some of whom are called "seers" (see Mosiah 8:13-18) who can see the evil in things the adversary promotes as harmless. Prophets do us no good unless we are willing to listen to them. They have consistently spoken out against heavy metal concerts, Rave parties, drug use, pornography, violent movies, and songs and movies which glorify immorality, lawlessness, and disregard for the sacred. These things are not mentioned by name in the scriptures, so people are left to wonder what is "right" unless we listen to and keep our eyes on the living prophets.

At times the counsel from our prophet leaders is uncomfortable because it runs against what we would like to do. The only safety we have in the battle against Satan is to follow the prophets until it becomes clear why they are counseling us as they are. Many times over my lifetime I have had to follow prophetic counsel not fully understanding the reason behind their warnings. Only later has it become evident. Too many of my acquaintances have refused to follow counsel because they didn't see the logic in it. Some have paid with their lives. Others have gone through a lot of unnecessary sorrow and heartache as they learned the true meaning of the Lord's declaration "whether by mine own voice or by the voice of my servants, it is the same" (D&C 1:38).

During these turbulent times, your safety and mine depend on how carefully we listen to and follow the inspired counsel of our leaders. Search the scriptures for examples (not a few!) of individuals and nations who chose to disregard prophetic warnings and were destroyed. Can we learn to be more wise than they?

Next, Paul urges us to have "your feet shod with the preparation of the gospel of peace" (Ephesians 6:15). President Lee compares our feet to our goals. What does it mean to have on our shoes preparing us for the gospel of peace? Who is the "Prince of Peace?" Christ! Where is He? In the highest degree of the Celestial Kingdom. So if our sights (goals) are set on the highest degree of the Celestial Kingdom, most of the difficult decisions of life will be easily made. All one has to do is ask: "If I do (say, think, act, recreate, drink, participate in, etc.) this activity, will it take me closer to or further away from my goal of going to the highest degree of the Celestial Kingdom?" Almost always, the answer will be obvious. If it takes you further away (no matter whether it is a little detour or a huge diversion from the "straight and narrow path") then don't do it! It is just that easy.

For example, you know that in order to go to the highest degree of the Celestial Kingdom you must be married in the temple (see D&C 131:1-4). Therefore, in choosing people to date you simply ask the question: "Is this person worthy and willing to go with me to the temple?" You may think you are only "dating for fun," but over a lifetime I have seen too many marriages outside the temple which started with just a "fun date"—nothing serious, something you can break off any time, but it evolves into love which then clouds reasoning and diverts goals from a life-long planned temple marriage.

If I really have my feet shod with the preparation of the gospel of peace, where will I be every Sunday? What will be the first thing I take from each paycheck? How will my DVD, video, or movie choices be affected? How will I dress during the hot days of summer? What will I be doing (if I'm a boy) when I reach the age of nineteen? The list goes on and on. Can't you see that life is greatly simplified if you have made certain goals early and then allow those goals to dictate what activities you will and will not participate in?

Paul continues "And take the helmet of salvation" (Ephesians 6:17). President Lee states the obvious — the helmet covers the head, which is the intellect. Our intellect is protected by our understanding and acceptance of the Plan of Salvation. If you ever forget who you are ( a child of God born to become like your Eternal Parents); where you came from (the presence of God after a long pre-mortal life of intense training for Godhood); why you are here (to get a body, gain the necessary ordinances, keep the commandments so you can return to live eternally with our Father); where you are going (the post-mortal spirit world to await the resurrection); and where you will spend eternity (in whichever kingdom of glory you have earned the right to live based on the laws you have chosen to live), then Satan can easily divert your attention to things which are "fun" but of no eternal value.

Once Satan penetrates your "helmet of salvation" (your belief and acceptance of the plan of salvation), you have no incentive to stay morally clean, to avoid the enticing entertainment of the world, or to pay the price to achieve eternal goals. Probably the fastest way to destroy Latter-day Saint youth (and adults!) is to flood their minds with the humanistic philosophies of the world. Your "primo-genator" (first father) was not some scum on the top of a prehistoric pond, according to what you are taught daily in your science classes. Your Primo-genator is God! Given that offspring grow up to be like their parents, can you see the huge difference? If scum is your original father, you'll grow up like that. If God is your First Father, then you have the ability to grow up to be like Him. There couldn't be a greater difference.

Given that you are covered with the semi-permanent armor, there is yet one more piece of defensive armor. Paul urges us: "Above all, taking the shield of faith, wherewith ye shall be able to quench all the fiery darts of the wicked" (Ephesians 6:16). A shield is used wherever you are being attacked! If your belief in the plan of salvation is faltering, move your shield to protect your head. If you really don't know where dinosaurs fit into earth's history, have perfect faith that God does and that He will someday reveal it to us (see D&C 101:32-34). You may not fully understand why you can't smoke marijuana but God does and you can have complete faith that in the end you will see the Divine wisdom in His counsel to avoid it. That shield of faith doubles your protection when coupled with the breastplate of righteousness. You may not understand why you can't be more sexually involved with your girlfriend (or boyfriend) before you are married, since we are to get to know each other in all areas, but you can have a sure knowledge that God understands and has required us to wait for a purpose that goes far beyond anything you can comprehend. So it is in all areas. You can move your shield to whatever area where the devil is buffeting you. I guess if I'm being beat up all over, I can curl up beneath the shield until the temptations pass.

Interestingly, there is one part of the body not protected by the defensive armor– the back! I suspect that is because we must meet our temptations face on. No running away from them. But even if you have all of these parts of the armor, Satan will eventually break through and destroy you unless you have an offensive weapon. Paul states that the offensive weapon is: "the sword of the Spirit, which is the word of God" (Ephesians 6:17). To Joseph Smith the Lord clarifies "the sword of my Spirit, which I will pour out upon you, and my word which I reveal unto you" (D&C 27:18).

Our only hope for victory is living well enough to have the Spirit with us. If we lie to our leaders as we fill out our missionary papers, if we are not totally truthful when we get our temple recommend, if we attempt to deceive our leaders in the MTC and the mission field, we forfeit our right to the Spirit. Then we enter the battle field without an offensive weapon and it will only be a matter of time before the adversary will inflict a mortal wound that will result in our returning home early and without honor.

Don't be so foolish as to believe that Satan can't or won't take full advantage as he seeks to destroy you. You must establish now the practice of feeding your spirit daily by reading and studying the scriptures. Starve your body and it will wither and eventually die. Starve your spirit by refusing to feed it the word of God and it will suffer the same fate. If you are wise enough to "put on the whole armor of God" you may be able to withstand the evil day. If you are not, the outcome will be sure and painful. Do what you must to insure that you are fully clothed and protected before entering the major battle field of mortality — the mission field.

*Chapter 15*

# YOUR KEYS TO SUCCESS – OBEDIENCE AND DILIGENCE

It seems that everyone is loaded with the "key to success" in whatever venture you are engaged. However, let's look to the scriptures and the prophets to see what God has declared to be the keys to success here and hereafter. The Lord revealed: "There is a law, irrevocably decreed in heaven before the foundations of this world, upon which all blessings are predicated — And when we obtain any blessing from God, it is by obedience to that law upon which it is predicated" (D&C 130:20-21). Thus it seems fairly clear that virtually every blessing in this life depends on our obedience to the law upon which that blessing is predicated. The same thing would hold true for the opposite side of the coin. There is a law irrevocably decreed in heaven before the foundations of this world, upon which all cursings are predicated — and when we are cursed of God, it is by disobedience to the Divinely given law.

If you want a blessing from God (e.g. success on your mission, in marriage, or in life), then all you have to do instigate the desired blessing is determine the law upon which it is predicated, obey that law, and the promised blessing will be yours. It is unreasonable to believe that God, who became what He is by obedience to law, would break His own laws and bestow unearned eternal blessings upon His children.

The Lord further revealed: "I, the Lord, am bound when ye do what I say; but when ye do not what I say, ye have no promise" (D&C 82:10). So determine what kind of missionary you want to be, obey the law upon which it is predicated, and you'll be that kind of a missionary. I became irritated when missionaries would "wish" they were something else. The desired blessings of mortality or eternity will not be received because of a "wish" or a "hope" with little or no effort on our part.

If you are obedient, you can (with confidence) expect that the promised blessings will be yours. In addition to the commandments which are written in the scriptures and the counsel of living prophets, you have the "white bible" or Missionary Handbook. Some missionaries take a "pick and choose" approach to the directives given in the missionary handbook. What a terrible mistake. The Lord never did say: "I the Lord am bound if you do at least 80% of what I say. And you can expect full blessings when you are partially obedient!" That would violate eternal laws, at which point "God would cease to be God" (see Alma 42:13).

There are two ways which obedience is achieved — one is promoted by Satan and the other is God's method. Satan would have all the controls on how one acts come from the outside — let someone else be responsible for how you act. That kind of control requires that there be a law for every situation. If there is no law or no one there to enforce the existing law, then the person controlled by law is totally out of control. Prisons are filled with people who have bought into this kind of control.

Unfortunately, too many preparing missionaries seem to have the same mistaken philosophy. If their parents don't catch them then they feel they are free to act as they want. If their bishop or teacher doesn't "nail" them then they got away with something. If you are unfortunate enough to have a missionary companion who still lives under this very childish mentality, you will come to know too soon how annoying they can be.

Some people never grow out of the "control coming from the outside" philosophy. They will never achieve their eternal potential until they shed that Satan-inspired way of being forced to obey. Who do you think controls God's behavior? The obvious answer is, "He controls Himself!" How can we ever become like Him if we expect others to monitor and control our behavior?

The second philosophy for control is God's way. When asked how he was able to govern such a large group of people, the Prophet Joseph Smith said: "I teach them correct principles, and they govern themselves" (as quoted by President Spencer W. Kimball in *The Teachings of Spencer W. Kimball*, p.191). No need for someone to "make your mind," or look over your shoulder, or force you to be good. Once a God-centered person knows the correct principle, the control comes from within! Where do you stand in how you are governed? By others from the outside? Or by yourself — where the control comes from within?

The huge difference is, when a person who is controlled from the outside doesn't have a specific law to meet the situation, he or she is totally out of control. When the control comes from the inside (because he or she knows the correct principle), the person is never out of control.

One P-day I received a phone call from an upset junior companion. His senior companion had arranged to go sky-diving for their P-day activity and the younger missionary was concerned. He called me to make sure it wasn't breaking a mission rule. I requested to talk with the senior companion (a missionary who had not made the transition to "principle-based" control). The senior immediately started to defend his decision by stating that nothing in the white handbook forbade them from skydiving. I asked him to read from pages 22 and 23 of the White Handbook. It reads that "recreational activities should be safe and low risk." I asked if jumping out of an airplane at 10,000 feet was safe. He assured me that it was since the parachute would be tethered to the plane and open automatically. Continuing to read, it states: "Do not engage in contact sports, water sports, winter sports, motorcycling, horse-back riding, mountain climbing, riding in private boats or airplanes, etc." I asked him how he was going to get up to 10,000 feet. He said a ward member had a plane and would fly them up. I asked whether it was a Delta airplane or a United airplane? He said it was the member's private plane. Only then did it dawn on him that he would be breaking the mission rules by skydiving.

Any missionary in the mind set of "control from within" would know that skydiving violated the principle of P-day activities even if it didn't break the law. Needless to say, they didn't go skydiving!

If you are still in the habit of trying to see how much you can get away with, you are sentencing yourself to many seasons of heartache and disappointment as well as very slow spiritual growth towards godhood, because you are not evolving into what God is — an Exalted Man who is completely and totally controlled by Self.

When the concept became cemented in my mind, I taught it to the mission and also to my own family members. Whenever a child (or missionary) would get out of line, I merely had to give them "that look." My oldest son, at the time a young teenager, would look at me and say: "I know dad, 'the control is better when it comes from within!'" To which I would reply: "Then control yourself!" It was amazing how little discipline I had to administer because both our own children and the missionaries already knew the right thing to do. Now they just needed to be reminded.

Would you like to prosper and have an abundance while most others are struggling during the troubled times before the Second Coming? The Lord said: "Behold, the Lord requireth the heart and a willing mind; and the willing and obedient shall eat the good of the land of Zion in these last days" (D&C 64:34).

If you are not obedient as a missionary, then the fulness of the Spirit will not be yours. Without the Spirit you will not be sensitive to the promptings of whom to talk to, where to proselyte, what areas to avoid, when to challenge an investigator to be baptized, and a thousand other things you do as a missionary. You may be the most diligent person in the mission field and still not prosper unless you are obedient.

The second key to success is diligence. The Lord said: "it is expedient that he should be diligent, that thereby he might win the prize; therefore, all things must be done in order" (Mosiah 4:27). The "prize" for missionary work is eternal life (see Mark 10:28-30). As you face the loneliness of the world, here is another great promise by the Lord to the diligent: "Be faithful and diligent in keeping the commandments of God, and I will encircle thee in the arms of my love" (D&C 6:20).

In order to continue the perfecting process, it is necessary to be diligent in all things. The Lord revealed: "And they shall also be crowned with blessings from above, yea, and with commandments not a few, and with revelations in their time — they that are faithful and diligent before me" (D&C 59:4). Thus the God-revealed key to receiving blessings from heaven, and also revelations from God, is diligence.

Even if you are obedient to all mission rules, if you are

not diligent enough to be where you ought to be, when you ought to be there, doing what you ought to be doing, then many faith-increasing experiences will pass you by. It became necessary one time to reprimand two missionaries who were staying in their apartment until the middle of the afternoon each day. When I confronted them, they explained that nothing was happening in their area during the morning hours and so in order to use their time more productively, they decided to stay home and study their scriptures. They told me how much they had learned that made them more effective missionaries.

I instructed them to obey the rules of the white handbook by getting out every day at 9:30 a.m. and staying out (except for an hour lunch period) until 9:30 p.m. I promised them that if they were diligent the Lord would bless their efforts. Reluctantly they agreed to follow my counsel. Miraculously, within a week they had found a golden family to teach (during a morning walk through the park!), they had helped several people with car problems (during the non-productive morning hours!), they had assisted with crowd control at the local elementary school during morning recess, they had been invited to teach a class in Mormon Doctrine to an American History class at the local high school — during the first period of the day. The list went on, but you get the point. As they followed the rules and were diligently applying themselves to the work, the Lord opened the windows of heaven and poured out blessings that had been there all the time but had been missed because the missionaries were not diligent.

It is a sad commentary on the lasting effects of a mission to see recently returned missionaries come home and take an ultra-casual approach to attending their church meetings, fulfilling their church callings, keeping the commandments, attending the temple, and striving for eternal life. If you can learn to be diligent during the entirety of your mission, then you'll have established a habit or pattern of diligence that will enable you to be where you ought to be, doing what you ought to be doing in the future so that the multitude of Divinely appointed blessings can be yours.

I wonder what disappointment we will experience when we stand with the Savior to review our mortal lives and discover what we could have enjoyed if we had been obedient to the commandments and diligent in our assigned tasks. You can avoid that embarrassing and regretful experience if you decide now to "put your shoulder to the wheel, push along!"

Look to our prophet leaders for examples of diligence and obedience. Although many of them are advancing in age and have been in their callings for many years, they set the pattern for diligence and obedience that we all can follow. Look to your bishop and stake president and you will see that you don't need to be an apostle or the prophet in order to be diligent and obedient. Likely your bishop is the busiest man in the ward and yet he also seems to be the happiest. By being diligent and obedient, we too can be happy, active, and filled with the spirit of our calling.

*Chapter 16*

# ONE DAY AT A TIME
## (dealing with homesickness, discouragement)

Now the time has come that you have likely talked about, dreamed about, and anticipated for a lifetime. Actually, if the veil of forgetfulness, which deprives us of our memory of the pre-mortal past, were removed, you would see that you have anticipated this mission for thousands of years. The Prophet Joseph Smith taught, "Every man who has a calling to minister to the inhabitants of the world was ordained to that very purpose in the Grand Council of heaven before this world was" (*Teachings of the Prophet Joseph Smith*, p. 365).

There seems to be a prevailing idea, however, that missions are easy and fun. To the contrary, they are difficult and sometimes very unpleasant — but the overall rewards far outweigh the tough times. A well-served mission literally becomes the foundation for the rest of your life. You will teach your children and your grandchildren the vital lessons of life which you learned in the mission field. If you go expecting an unparalleled challenging experience, you will have the proper mind-set.

One mistake which many missionaries make is to try to live their entire mission at once. Resolve to handle each challenge as it comes, day by day. The Lord had this in mind when He taught, "Take therefore no thought for the morrow: for the morrow shall take thought for the things of itself. Sufficient unto the day is the evil thereof" (Matthew 6:34). I have watched with sorrow as some missionaries would count down the days until their mission was over only to discover, when the end finally came, that they wanted to continue the experience. Too many hours and days were wasted "looking beyond the mark" (see Jacob 4:14). You'll never be a young, single missionary again. Don't waste one minute planning, day-dreaming, talking about, or writing home about what you will do after your mission. The only exception may be making application for re-admittance to school. Even then, your parents can do most of the leg work so you won't be distracted from your mission.

Even though you may be confident that you won't suffer homesickness, you likely will. Even if you are one of the few who don't, you will probably have companions who will. Understanding homesickness and how to overcome it could save your mission and prevent wasting precious time focused on yourself.

Homesickness can happen any time from when you are dropped off at the MTC to the end of your mission. You will recognize it when you wake up one morning before dawn and have the definite feeling "I'm not cut out to be a missionary. I need to go home!" Almost everyone (including your mission president!) has experienced that feeling. Satan would prompt you to mistakenly believe that you are the only one who has ever experienced what you are going through. Not true!

Homesickness can happen when you are thrust into a new environment (the MTC or a new area in the mission field), when you get a companion who isn't to your liking, when you realize that the language they taught in the MTC isn't remotely like what the native people speak, so you can neither speak to nor understand them. It may happen when your system rebels against the strange and exotic foods you are expected to eat. It may occur or recur when a close family member dies, when your family takes a vacation without you or gathers for a special holiday celebration. It might be more pronounced when a brother or sister or close friend gets married. It might sneak up on you when you receive a "Dear John" letter. It may happen if you become ill or if you are assigned to a difficult area where people are not very receptive. If you know it is likely to happen, then you can prepare mentally to combat it. But how?

First, homesickness comes because you are focused on your own needs and concerns rather than on those you are called to serve. Refusing to look inward can be all that is necessary to overcome feelings of homesickness. You need to understand that you won't be homesick for more than a week or two. If it goes longer than that, you'll terminate your mission and come home. So it isn't just a nice thing to overcome homesickness — it is a must.

The second you realize you are homesick, get down on your knees and tell our Heavenly Father about your feelings. He already knows, but there is something in admitting it to Him that begins the recovery process. Then get up from your knees and start to serve. Serve your companion (you could polish his shoes, press her dress, fix breakfast, or clean the apartment). You might look carefully at the members in the ward or branch where you are assigned. There will always be those who could use a word of encouragement, a helping hand in doing yard work, painting a fence, repairing a garage, or any of a thousand other little projects. Put on a happy face and greet people you meet on the street. Focus on what you have that makes your life good and try to identify areas where the gospel can enrich others lives. Volunteer at the elementary school for "crowd control" at recess or to tutor those who are struggling to learn to read. You might give service at the hospital or rest home. Playing checkers with an elderly person — let them win occasionally! — might seem like a waste of time to you, but it may be seen as a miracle by those you serve.

Obey all mission rules. It may seem strange, but too many of our missionaries, when they were fighting homesickness, confessed that they had broken a mission rule "just because they didn't care any more!" What a counterproductive thing to do. How can we expect the blessings of Heaven in overcoming homesickness when we refuse to follow the directions Heavenly Father has given us?

President Ezra Taft Benson said,

> I have often said one of the greatest secrets of missionary work is work! If a missionary works, he will get the Spirit; if he gets the Spirit, he will teach by the Spirit; and if he teaches by the Spirit, he will touch the hearts of the people and he will be happy. There will be no homesickness, no worrying about families, for all time and talents and interests are centered on the work of the ministry. Work, work, work—there is no satisfactory substitute, especially in missionary work. (Texas San Antonio Mission, 2 March 1986, *Teachings of Ezra Taft Benson*, p.200)

Don't let homesickness ruin the mission you have earned the right to serve through countless years of pre-mortal diligence. Resolve now that when those feelings come, you will recognize them for what they are, take a proactive approach in overcoming them, and redouble your efforts to help others avoid the devastation that will come if you return home early because of homesickness.

You are in a prime environment for discouragement or even some depression. Often we hold up the sons of Mosiah as the model of what kind of missionaries we want to be. However, their fourteen year mission was not easy and they were not always bubbling with enthusiasm. At the conclusion of their mission, they recorded, "Now **when our hearts were depressed, and we were about to turn back**, behold, the Lord comforted us, and said: Go amongst thy brethren, the Lamanites, and bear with patience thine afflictions, and **I will give unto you success**" (Alma 26:27, emphasis added). The Lord would say the same thing to you when you were ready to quit and return to your home. He wants you to be successful and has promised that He will be with you. Note these few scriptures: "Yet you should have been faithful; and he would have extended his arm and supported you against all the fiery darts of the adversary; and he **would have been with you in every time of trouble**" (D&C 3:8, emphasis added). "And whoso receiveth you, there I will be also, for I will go before your face. I will be on your right hand and on your left, and my Spirit shall be in your hearts, and mine angels round about you, to bear you up" (D&C 84:88). "And their arm shall be my arm, and I will be their shield and their buckler; and I will gird up their loins, and they shall fight manfully for me; and their enemies shall be under their feet; and I will let fall the sword in their behalf, and by the fire of mine indignation will I preserve them" (D&C 35:14).

Could I just list twenty-two things you might try when the spirit of discouragement and depression creeps up on you? Each one could be enlarged upon and I would suggest you spend some time expanding on each one so you can make it a tool in your chest to fight depression. It is true you will be in discouraging situations, but it doesn't follow that you must become discouraged. That is a choice you and you alone can make.

**1. Pray more earnestly** (Matthew 26:36-39; Mark 14:32-41; Luke 22:39-46). Even the Savior when He was faced with His greatest trial (Gethsemane and the cross), increased the intensity of His prayers.

**2. Read the Scriptures to get a more eternal perspective** (D&C 98:1-3; D&C 121:7-8; D&C 122:7-9; Joshua 1:6, 7, 9, 18). You'll discover that many of your scriptural heros had periods of discouragement but made it through and now their struggles are forgotten because of their successes — so will yours be!

**3. Honestly evaluate your life to see if un-repented sins are causing your depressed feelings.** You cannot do bad and feel good. Now with your focus almost entirely on spiritual self-improvement, it is common to see little sins you may have overlooked before. I'm not referring to the little sins of long ago. I'm focusing on those rather large sins you know you haven't taken care of before your mission.

**4. Learn from, deal with, and let go of the past — the future lies ahead, not behind!** You cannot go back and "un-sin," so you must either repent and move on or you'll eventually pay for your sins as the Savior did (see D&C 19:15-19). No matter what the past was, if you have repented you need to let go of it and move ahead with your life. Read carefully the apostle Paul's formula for ridding yourself of the past: "Brethren, I count not myself to have apprehended: but this one thing I do, forgetting those things which are behind, and reaching forth unto those things which are before, I press toward the mark for the prize of the high calling of God in Christ Jesus" (Philippians 3:13-14).

**5. Know yourself well enough to recognize when you are starting to slip into a depressed state. It may require spending some practice time with yourself.** Unless you know what is normal for you, how can you detect when something is definitely wrong? If you are perceptive, you'll learn to recognize when you are starting to slip.

**6. Have an already agreed upon plan to pull yourself up. What works for others may not work for you. Again, you must know yourself well enough to know what works for YOU.** What is effective in stopping the free-fall for others, may not work for you in pulling you out of a pre-depressive state. Experiment with different depression-dispelling tactics and see which ones work for you.

**7. Turn your focus outward. Get outside yourself and SERVE others.** Almost exclusively, in our mission, those who were depressed had taken the light that they had been given to lead others to Christ and focused it in their own eyes. Keep your focus outward and the pressing needs of your life will be taken care of by others.

**8. Avoid ALL negative self-talk. No "pity parties."** Too many people have fallen into the trap of telling themselves how bad they are. We literally become self-fulfilling prophecies. If you have the habit of putting yourself down, isn't today a great day to stop that self-destructive habit forever?

**9. Retreat to your sacred grove (physically if you can, mentally if you can't get away).** In the mission field, you will be on the treadmill of life and it will be going fast. Occasionally, you need to step off the tread mill, take a deep breath, and refocus your attention. Your sacred grove can be anywhere physical or mental where you can retreat to regroup. Find a sacred grove anywhere you go — you'll need one

**10. "Count Your Many Blessings" (mentally , physically or out loud if you must). "Name them one by one."See the blessings in everything.** Too often missionaries focus on what isn't going right rather than on what is going right. As you search for the positive in everything that happens to you, you'll find that virtually every black cloud has a silver lining. Without focusing on the black clouds, take time to thank the Lord for the silver linings.

**11. Get a priesthood blessing (listen to the promises and directives — spoken and unspoken). You may get more than one blessing for the same trial if you desire (see Mark 8:22-26).** Don't harbor the fear of depleting the power of the priesthood. If you feel you need extra help coping with the trials of a mission or life, get all the help you can. Far too often the greatest misuse of the priesthood comes from our lack of using it.

**12. Tackle one problem at a time. Don't try to fix everything all at once. Perfection will require the next life to achieve.** As the Spirit gets stronger in your life, your vision of what you want to become increases and intensifies. You'll want to be perfect "right now!" It isn't going to happen, so don't get discouraged when you discover that you still have a long way to go, even when your full-time mission is complete.

**13. Recognize and commend any and all progress. (God called every step of the creation — even though incomplete — "good" — see Moses 2:4, 10, 12, 18, 21, 25, 31 = "very good," when completed).** One of Satan's most effective tools is to convince you that you aren't making any progress. Perhaps that's why he is called "a liar from the beginning" (D&C 93:25). Nothing generates enthusiasm for the battle like a little success. Be willing to commend yourself in the small victories you achieve or the small steps forward.

**14. Talk courage and perseverance — not gloom and doom.** In a darkening and dismal world, it isn't easy to remain optimistic, but it is possible. Don't be artificial in either your happiness or optimism, be genuine. However, you must remember that though the progress you and the work are making may not be readily observable, both you and the work are destined to succeed. Temporary setbacks are just that — "temporary." I really believe what the Lord said: "Search diligently, pray always, and be believing, and all things shall work together for your good" (D&C 90:24).

**15. Re-read your patriarchal blessing (note gifts, promises, warnings, directives). Listen to the Spirit as it reads to you blessings written between the lines.** Some people are displeased with their blessings because they seem generic or common. However, if one views the patriarchal blessings as a catalyst for opening the revelatory windows of heaven, then as you read, the Spirit spreads the words in the sentences and separates the lines and allows the Lord to inspire you in what you need for that very moment. I would suggest you photo-reduce your blessing, laminate it, and carry it in your scriptures. Then read it often and note how it changes with each new situation you face that requires revelation to solve.

**16. Write a letter to a depressed friend, give counsel to help ease his burden. Wait to send it. Re-read it and the answer to your problem will be in the counsel you give.** One of the surprising things many missionaries reported was that as they wrote to friends or family at home, giving counsel to overcome their challenges, as they re-read the very counsel they gave, the Spirit would whisper to them "that is the answer to your problem!" Try it and see if it works for you.

**17. Physical Exercise — Use it to dissipate depression-causing toxins.** Exercise physiologists have identified certain toxins which are always present in depressed people. They have also discovered that rigorous exercise dissipates those toxins and often eliminates the depressive feelings. ~~You should have a regular exercise program and religiously stick to it.~~ Contact your mission president as to whether you may join a health club. A healthy missionary is a lot less likely to suffer debilitating discouragement than one who is out of shape.

**18. Listen to good, wholesome, uplifting music.** Good music is like a prayer to God (see D&C 25:12) and will be followed with blessings on your head. What better blessing than the power to overcome the depressive spirit? Your mission president will inform you what is and is not appropriate music. Do yourself a favor and eliminate those tunes you know will not be allowed in the mission field. Certain music invites the Spirit of the Lord and other music drives the Spirit away. If you are honest with yourself, you'll readily recognize the difference.

**19. Keep hanging on. Outlast the depressive spirit while doing everything you can.** Sometimes we have the mistaken idea that we ought to be instantly happy, never depressed, always on top, and continually in control of our emotions. When that doesn't happen, we tend to become concerned that we have offended God or are not living righteously enough to merit divine protection from the influences of the adversary. That is not true. Even the Savior faced times of discouragement and depression (see Matthew 27:37-38, Mark 14:33-34, also the footnote for verse 33). You can make it through although at times you'll be convinced that you can't. God didn't send you out to fail, and with His help you won't fail.

**20. Remember — The Book of Mormon is true!! About half the verses state a life-preserving truth: "It came to pass..." It did not come to stay!** I remember reading the Book of Mormon before my mission. I became intrigued with the beginning of so many verses which stated that "it came to pass." Although in later years I realized this was a literary style of the Hebrew language, the point was still there — our problems and trials are only temporary. They are not intended to be lasting. So when difficult times come, and come they will, remember that if you grit your teeth and hang on, the trials will pass, a brighter day will dawn, and everything will work out according to the Lord's plan for you and those among whom you serve.

**21. Follow the advice of the prophets.** You may not have listened too carefully to general conference speakers before your mission. However, in the mission field, you'll soon discover that they really are not just old men who are not in touch with what is going on. They are living prophets through whom God speaks in these latter days. They give counsel to meet and defeat every fiery dart of the adversary. They mark the pathway to peace in this life and eternal life in the world to come. You could do nothing better than develop a love affair with the messages of the living prophets while serving your mission. It will be a vital key to your survival both spiritual and physical during these days leading up to the Second Coming of the Savior.

**22. Get help from the mission president.** If you have tried all twenty-one of the above suggestions and you still cannot shake off the depressive spirit, then call the mission president for help. Never go longer than a week feeling down. For those of you who seldom if ever suffer from depression, you might call long before the week is up. For others who fight depressive feelings on a regular basis, a week may be about right.

If the mission president sends you to a counselor or a doctor who prescribes medication, then follow his counsel. The most important issue is your mental, physical, and spiritual well-being. When you are mentally balanced, physically in good shape, and spiritually in-tune with the Holy Ghost, you are poised to be the most effective missionary in the field. When one or more of those three areas is out of balance, then you diminish your effectiveness. Be a modern warrior for the Lord by being prepared for the frontal attack by the adversary which could blind-side you into believing that you cannot be a successful missionary.

*Chapter 17*

# IF YE ARE NOT ONE –
# COMPANIONSHIP
# RELATIONSHIPS

The Lord is very emphatic: " I say unto you, be one; and if ye are not one ye are not mine" (D&C 38:27). As we will discuss later as we examine the satanic opposition you will face, one of the titles by which Satan is known is "the enemy of all righteousness" (Alma 34:23). Therefore it should be expected that the devil will try everything in his power to drive a wedge between companions, thus putting them outside the protective umbrella of being one with God.

Unfortunately for us, Satan does not wait until we are in the mission field. He starts working on us while we are still young children, trying to get us to "transgress the laws of God, and fight and quarrel one with another, and serve the devil, who is the master of sin, or who is the evil spirit which hath been spoken of by our fathers, he being an enemy to all righteousness" (Mosiah 4:14).

If you are still living at home while reading this book, or if you are living in with others in an apartment at school, you have an opportunity to begin early to master this

Christ-like trait of getting along with others. If you are already serving your mission, then it will require that you get your experience in "on the job training."

From the time we were little babies, we summoned others to meet our needs by crying and fussing. Although we were unable to communicate using words, we could make our wants known and grew to expect that others would put aside whatever they were doing to tend to our needs. Unfortunately, too many missionaries fail to make the transition from being served to serving. As people mature and grow in strength and size, many discover that they can get their way by throwing temper tantrums. They become expert in knowing what works and what doesn't, when they can get away with a tantrum and when they are punished for their childish behavior, and what issues are important enough to engage in manipulative behavior and which ones are not.

I have asked college-age students how long they thought it would take to "push their parents' buttons" and make them angry if the winner were to receive $1,000? One young man enthusiastically shout, "give me two seconds and I can make my parents raging mad!" I could tell he was speaking from experience. Then I ask, "If you know how to do it, why would you?" Is our objective to irritate and make angry? Again, the scriptures reveal that one of Satan's tactics is to "stir them up to anger" (see D&C 10:24). So, as we consciously try to make people angry or mad, we are literally becoming a tool in Satan's hands.

If you have been deceived into such a practice either with your parents, siblings, or friends, this looks like a great time to abandon that satanic behavior and start practicing how to be a peacemaker. Remember in the Sermon on the Mount the Savior taught, "Blessed are the peacemakers: for they shall be called the children of God" (Matthew 5:9).

Because Satan is generally not successful in getting

missionaries to break the mission-ending commandments, he must look elsewhere to neutralize their effectiveness. Most often that comes in the form of ill feelings between companions. My experience has been that the companions seldom argue and fight over "right and wrong" issues. It is generally over matters of personal preference. When a missionary (or person) demands to have things his way all the time, others soon tire of that selfishness and then the power struggle begins. At first it may be in the form of jesting or teasing. Soon it escalates into harsh words and accusations. If not discontinued, it can result in physical confrontation where one or both companions are injured. Unless hearts are softened and apologies offered and accepted, Satan has just succeeded in destroying a companionship. What a shame. It may be that you could have been the most powerful companionship in the mission, but now you must be separated to prevent further violence.

If you mistakenly believe that you can bully your way through the family, with your friends, and at school, and then instantaneously change into a loving, easy-to-be-entreated missionary, you are only deceiving yourself. What you are and how you have learned to solve problems will surface almost immediately when you enter the MTC and the mission field. I saw young men and women with almost unlimited potential who never amounted to anything as missionaries because they refused to learn to become one with their companions.

Although this book is not about marriage, it would be too bad not to finish the scenario of the demanding, tempter tantrum missionary. I have been home from being a mission president long enough to see what happens to missionaries who refuse to learn to be one with their companions. Sister Bott and I attended literally hundreds of our missionaries' temple weddings when we were released. Never once did we enter the temple and have the couple say, "Oh, we're marrying for time and all eternity, but if things get tough, we plan to divorce!" But it has become an unhappy reality that several of those former missionaries have divorced. As we have tried to evaluate the cause of the divorce, not infrequently the conclusion is that they never learned how to give and take with their companions in the mission field. When they tried to carry that same bullying, selfish tactic into marriage, the wife or husband refused to tolerate such childish behavior. Rather than change, the stubborn returned missionary gave up their dream for an eternal marriage. What a shame that such an easy lesson couldn't be learned and mastered long before kneeling at the altar in the temple.

As painful as it may be, today would not be too soon to honestly evaluate yourself and see if you are guilty of trying to get your way by force, tantrum, bullying, or sulking. If you must honestly answer "yes" to the question, save yourself, your future companions, your future wife or husband and children the pain of living with a person who tries to use satanic means to get his or her way in life.

How do you do it? You might start by trying to see life through the other person's eyes. How would you feel if you were in their position? That one question alone will modify the way you do missionary work. How would you feel (or do you feel!) when someone attacks your religion without any real understanding of what they are talking about? How presumptuous! Yet I find myself doing essentially the same thing. I have several very educated friends in England who are staunch Roman Catholics. I have to consciously check myself to make sure I'm not trying to tell them what their church believes.

On a lower level, you might ask yourself, "How would I feel if someone used the same tactics I use on other people against me?" With road rage on the rise, I often wonder out loud to my wife how the person who just cut me off would react if I did the same thing to him? The news reports of fights, shootings, and car wrecks answer the question.

If your answer is that you wouldn't be happy at all being treated by others as you treat them, then you are seeing the present day application of the Golden Rule: "Therefore all things whatsoever ye would that men should do to you, do ye even so to them: for this is the law and the prophets" (Matthew 7:12).

Although I know it sounds a little Primary-like, the principle is completely celestial. You might now ask yourself: "What would Jesus do?" As a full time missionary, you are literally a stand-in for the Savior. You must do as He would do, talk as He would talk, act as He would act, think as He would think, and be as He is. As a resurrected Being, He said, "what manner of men ought ye to be? Verily I say unto you, even as I am" (3 Nephi 27:27). How can you, therefore, be a stand-in for the Savior if your behavior is opposite from His?

Next comes the lofty goal of serving an honorable mission. The prerequisites for service in His kingdom are outlined in Doctrine and Covenants 4:5-6: "And faith, hope, charity and love, with an **eye single to the glory of God**, qualify him for the work.

"Remember faith, virtue, knowledge, temperance, patience, brotherly kindness, godliness, charity, humility, diligence" (emphasis added). Of the five qualifers mentioned in verse 5, we often assume we understand the first four. However, what does serving with "an eye single to the glory of God" mean? You will recall that the Lord defines His work and His glory in Moses 1:39: "For behold, this is my work and my glory — to bring to pass the immortality and eternal life of man."

Therefore, if your eye is single to His glory then

everything you do to, with, and for your fellowmen is designed to lift them, perfect them, and prepare them for eternal life. So the next step is no more difficult than asking yourself: "If I do, say, think, act towards others in the way I am planning, will it make them a better person? Will they be better prepared for the celestial kingdom? Will I be helping or hindering them?" The answer to those questions will dictate whether your actions are Christ-like or not.

You can readily see that acting in a Christ-like manner is not a state you will arrive at overnight. However, the sooner you start the sooner you'll arrive. If you have ever had the opportunity to interact with an apostle or church leader, you'll immediately sense what it is like to be treated in a Christ-like way. Although you may not be perfect to begin with, by consciously trying you'll discover that your whole outlook on your fellow human beings will change. You'll start to see every person on earth as a brother or a sister. You will look beyond the way they dress, the tattoos and body piercings, the addictions, and the bad language. Looking beyond the physical appearance and into their hearts and souls, you'll start to see them as God sees them and then you'll discover it is infinitely easier to love and serve them.

The whole of the gospel is easier to live and apply when you view it from a Christ-like perspective. Are you too young to start? If you are reading this book, you are not too young. Have you gone too far because of past mistakes to make it back and become a Christ-like missionary? The Savior said: "Wherefore I say unto you, All manner of sin and blasphemy shall be forgiven unto men: but the blasphemy against the Holy Ghost shall not be forgiven unto men" (Matthew 12:31).

As you consciously strive to be one with your family, friends, relatives, and acquaintances, you will find the power of the Holy Ghost assisting you in overcoming past habits and urging you onward. Your life is ahead of you. Take control and become as Jesus was and earn the same reward that Jesus earned — eternal life.

*Chapter 18*

# HOW TO RECOGNIZE ANSWERS TO PRAYER

Almost all the remainder of the book will be devoted to helping you see the doctrine of the Church in a way that will enhance your ability to apply it in your own life and teach it to others as a missionary. Books have and will be written on each one of these topics. Therefore, this will not be a comprehensive investigation of the doctrine but rather an overview.

One of the most confusing topics discussed in my Missionary Preparation and Doctrine and Covenants classes is: "How do I tell if I'm answering my own prayers?" Even the returned missionaries in the Doctrine and Covenants classes take a lot of notes and ask a lot of questions. If you don't know how to recognize the answer to prayers yourself, then how can you teach your investigators to recognize when they have that confirming witness or answer to their prayers about the truthfulness of the gospel?

The Lord said: "If thou shalt ask, thou shalt receive revelation upon revelation, knowledge upon knowledge, that thou mayest know the mysteries and peaceable things

169

— that which bringeth joy, that which bringeth life eternal" (D&C 42:61). But how does one ask and receive revelation? Perhaps we can use Oliver Cowdery's example as a model for us.

Oliver was staying with the Smiths in the Palmyra, New York area because, as a teacher, part of his pay was to room and board with the parents of the children who attended his school. One night after dinner the Smiths were sitting around the fire talking about things that were most important in their lives. Without the modern conveniences of electricity, television, radio, DVDs, etc., every night became a Family Night between dinner and bedtime. The things of greatest interest to the Smiths happened to be golden plates, Urim and Thummim, angels, and the translation of the Book of Mormon.

Fearing that he had fallen among religious fanatics, Oliver excused himself from the meeting and retired to his bedroom. There he knelt down and humbly asked God whether what was being discussed down stairs was true. Joseph Smith records that God showed Oliver in open vision that he [Joseph Smith] had the plates and that the translation was true (see *Papers of Joseph Smith* 1:10).

So convinced was Oliver that, at the end of the school year near the first of April, he left Palmyra and traveled to Harmony, Pennsylvania where Joseph and Emma Smith were living. He arrived on April 5, 1829, and on April 7th he began to act as scribe for Joseph as he translated the Book of Mormon. On that very day Oliver must have had some second thoughts. He went to Joseph and must have said something like: "Joseph, I want this work to be true more than anything else, but how can I be assured that I'm not answering my own prayers since I want it so badly?" Together they decided to ask the Lord for the desired clarification.

Doctrine and Covenants 6, 8, and 9 all deal with how to

recognize answers to prayers. Starting in Section 6 the Lord revealed: "Verily, verily, I say unto thee, blessed art thou for what thou hast done; for thou hast inquired of me, and behold, as often as thou hast inquired thou hast received instruction of my Spirit. If it had not been so, thou wouldst not have come to the place where thou art at this time" (D&C 6:14). "Inquired" is another way of saying "asked." The Lord seldom answers prayers that haven't been asked! As a missionary, make sure you remember to "Pray always, that you may come off conqueror; yea, that you may conquer Satan, and that you may escape the hands of the servants of Satan that do uphold his work" (D&C 10:5). Whenever a missionary was struggling more than normal, upon questioning he or she was not being diligent in saying their prayers.

Note carefully that "as often as thou hast inquired thou hast received instruction of my Spirit" — every single, sincere prayer is answered. Then our major problem isn't "getting" an answer to prayer but "recognizing" the method the Lord chooses to answer our prayer. The first sign that we are receiving answer to prayer comes in the remainder of verse 14: "If it had not been so, thou wouldst not have come..." **Answer to prayer always motivates to action!** When you feel prompted it may just be a thought or an impression. It might be to visit a certain family or avoid traveling a certain street or teach a certain concept to an investigating family. Learn to follow those promptings.

Verse 15 provides the second way to recognize an answer to prayer. "Behold, thou knowest that thou hast inquired of me and I did **enlighten thy mind;** and now I tell thee these things that thou mayest know that thou hast been enlightened by the Spirit of truth" (D&C 6:15, emphasis added). The Prophet Joseph Smith taught,

> The Spirit of Revelation is in connection with these blessings. A person may profit by noticing the

first intimation of the spirit of revelation; for instance, when you feel pure intelligence flowing into you, it may give you sudden strokes of ideas, so that by noticing it, you may find it fulfilled the same day or soon; (i.e.,) those things that were presented unto your minds by the Spirit of God, will come to pass; and thus by learning the Spirit of God and understanding it, you may grow into the principle of revelation, until you become perfect in Christ Jesus. (*Teachings of the Prophet Joseph Smith*, p.151)

The Spirit (Who answers our prayers) "enlightens the mind and fills your soul with joy" (D&C 11:13). However, do you ever have the problem with your mind wandering while you are praying? I would find that as I was praying my mind would be off thinking about something else. Rather embarrassed, I would pull it back into the prayer, apologize to the Lord, and continue the prayer. Now I take a different approach. Let me illustrate the point:

Suppose you had a doctrinal question and couldn't find the answer. You decided to call me on the phone for some help. After asking your question, what would you do? I suspect you'd pause and wait for me to answer. I would think you were really strange, even rude, if, after asking the question, you continued talking and then hung up! How is it in prayer? We dial up God on the "cell phone" (i.e. celestial phone), thank Him for a list of blessings He gives us, order Him around heaven with His omnipotent power, then give Him a shopping list of questions we want answered and then — hang up!

I am just your spirit brother and am willing to honor your request for enlightenment when you ask. God is your Father — would He do any less? Why not pause after asking your question and allow the Lord time to immediately answer your question. If we listened carefully to what the Prophet Joseph Smith taught about "sudden strokes of ideas" and what the Lord said about "enlightening your mind," then we will happily discover that the Lord answers many of our prayers as soon as we ask. Be informed that some prayers are answered by a "no" and others may be put on "hold" until the time is right, but every single sincere prayer will be answered.

Before ending Section 6 the Lord gives one more clue how to recognize answers to prayers. After reminding Oliver of the experience he had in Palmyra the night he was troubled about what he had heard from the Smiths (see D&C 6:22), the Lord revealed: "Did I not speak **peace to your mind** concerning the matter? What greater witness can you have than from God?" (D&C 6:23 emphasis added). Only the Prince of Peace (Christ — Isaiah 9:6) can bring peace. Neither you or the devil can duplicate that inner peace of mind that passes all understanding.

Satisfied that he fully understood how to recognize answers to prayers and steadfast that he would never question again, Oliver must have thanked the Lord and been ready to move on. Two sections later, however, he was questioning again. He must have said: "How do I know I wasn't just talking myself into thinking I had an answer since I am accustomed to working things through intellectually?" The Lord patiently continues Oliver's tutoring.

> Yea, behold, **I will tell you in your mind and in your heart**, by the Holy Ghost, which shall come upon you and which shall dwell in your heart.
>
> Now, behold, this is the **spirit of revelation**; behold, this is the spirit by which Moses brought the children of Israel through the Red Sea on dry ground. (D&C 8:2-3, emphasis added)

Not "mind **OR** heart" but "mind **AND** heart" constitute the answer to prayer. Either you or the adversary can manipulate one domain (mind or heart) or the other, but neither you nor the adversary can manipulate them both. The Lord calls "mind AND heart" together **the spirit of revelation**. If anyone but God could use both domains at the same time, we would have no assurance that we weren't answering our own prayers!

Using Moses as an example, as he was leading the Children of Israel towards the promised land, we may ponder: "How did Moses know what to do when he was confronted with the Red Sea in front and Pharaoh's army behind?" I suspect when Moses realized the tough spot they were in (Red Sea in front, terrible army in the rear), he complained to God: "Dear God, You've got a real problem." To which the Lord likely said: "No Moses, you've got the problem! I'm up here and you're down there!" Moses then realized that he was expected to come up with a possible solution to the problem. He might have said: "Why don't You hold them off with a pillar of fire while we march around the end of the Red Sea. Then when we're opposite them, You can let them rush to the sea. We'll wave at them as we continue our journey into the desert." The Lord might have responded: "Good idea, Moses. Cast thine eyes to the left and to the right." Upon doing so, Moses would have discovered that the Red Sea is too large to quickly march around. Realizing that the option he had suggested wasn't viable, Moses probably thought really hard and then said: "Why don't we build rafts and float across the sea, leaving only sagebrush for them to use as rafts!" To which the Lord likely responded: "Good idea, Moses, which tree do you want to start with?" As Moses looked around, he discovered that there weren't any trees!

I'm sure this didn't happen, but what if Moses said, "Why don't we e-mail the president of the United States, he'll send the United States Navy over here. We'll lob some missiles over on old Pharaoh and his army and then we'll sail off into the sunset!" That would be a good modern day solution to the problem, to which the Lord would respond: "Good idea, Moses, if you want to wait 3,500 years!"

Probably in total frustration Moses said: "Well, why don't we just part the sea and walk straight through!" to which the Lord responded by confirming to Moses' mind AND heart that the decision he had arrived at was the right one. It really wasn't a common thing for people to part seas and walk through them. In fact, to this point in recorded history, it had never happened before. As Moses followed the "spirit of revelation," he commanded the sea to part and it obeyed. You know the rest of the story.

Now the Lord asks Oliver if he would like to translate to which Oliver excitedly answers "yes." After trying and failing (see D&C 9:5), Oliver dejectedly complains that translating didn't work and wanted to know why? The Lord explained: "Behold, you have not understood; you have supposed that I would give it unto you, when you took no thought save it was to ask me" (D&C 9:7). Too often people want the Lord to make their decisions for them. Answer this question: who makes decisions for the Lord? The obvious answer is: He makes His own. Where did He learn to make decisions? Certainly not by having His Father make His decisions. He learned while on an earth like us. If God made even the smallest decision for us, He would be robbing us of the growth-producing effects of learning to make decisions the Lord's way. He will prompt, inspire, guide, direct, and enlighten us in the right direction, but He will not make the decision for us.

A good key to remember is: whoever will ultimately stand judgment for the decision must make the decision. You can see the logic in that statement. It would be grossly unfair for someone else to make a decision for you and then you have to account for the consequences of that decision.

The Lord seems to say: "Don't worry, Oliver, this hasn't

been a wasted experience. I will use you as an example of what NOT to do from now to the Millennium!" Then the Lord instructs Oliver (and all of us) in the correct way. "But, behold, I say unto you, that you must study it out in your mind; then you must ask me if it be right, and if it is right I will cause that your bosom shall burn within you; therefore, you shall feel that it is right" (D&C 9:8). What is the "it" you must study out in your mind? Whatever the problem is you are facing or the decision you are required to make! What is the "it" you must ask is correct? The decision you, by your own mental exercise, have determined to be the correct thing to do! If the decision is correct, the Lord promises that He will "cause your bosom to burn within you," therefore you will know that your answer is right? NO! Then you shall "feel" the answer is right. Why not "know?" Because you have already done the intellectual work to "know" the answer. Now you must "feel" it– remember: "I will tell you in your mind AND in your heart" (D&C 8:2-3).

What if the decision you have made is wrong? Almost everyone, including returned missionaries, will say: "You will have a stupor of thought!" which is only half correct. If the Lord tells you "Yes" in your mind AND your heart, why would He tell you "no" only in your mind? Remember: either you or the devil can manipulate one domain or the other but neither you nor the devil can manipulate them both at the same time!

The Lord says: "But if it be not right you shall have **no such feelings**, but you shall have a **stupor of thought** that shall cause you to forget the thing which is wrong" (D&C 9:9, emphasis added). Another way of saying "cause you to forget" would be "shall turn your heart away" from the decision you have made. Melvin J. Ballard, an apostle who lived a number of years ago, taught: "'But if it be not right, you shall have no such feelings, but you shall have a stupor of thought that shall cause you to forget the thing which is wrong' that shall turn your heart away from the thing that you had contemplated" (*Conference Report*, April 1931, p. 37).

A quick story will summarize the points made in this chapter. A number of years ago I served as bishop of a singles ward at BYU. One day a twenty-seven year old single young man came to my office to renew his temple recommend. As he sat down I had a flash of thought cross my mind and asked: "Are you any closer to marriage today than you were six years ago when you returned from your mission?" He grimaced and said: "Gee, Bishop, I wish you would have asked me that question yesterday." I asked "why?" He said: "I just broke my fourth engagement yesterday." I asked: "Don't you love the girl?" to which he responded: "I worship the ground on which she walks." I continued: "Then why don't you marry her?" He said: "The Lord told me she is the wrong one!" I asked: "How do you know the Lord told you she was the wrong one?" He said: "It is always the same. We get engaged, have our pictures taken for the wedding announcements [and then he added "I don't know why the Lord waits until after the pictures are taken. It is awfully expensive!"], and then it happened again." Becoming somewhat frustrated, I asked: "What happened again?" He said: "When I got home yesterday I was sitting in my apartment pondering about being married to the girl of my dreams and I had a sudden wave of doubt and fear come over me and I knew the Lord was telling me this was not the right one!"

I said to him: "You jerk! Don't you know that God never uses doubt and fear as a negative answer?" He said: "Run that by me one more time, Bishop." I said: "God never uses doubt and fear as a negative answer. Then I quoted the following three scriptures: "For God hath not given us the spirit of fear; but of power, and of love, and of a sound mind" (2 Timothy 1:7). If "fear" doesn't come from God, where does it come from? If you answer "from the devil," you are correct. Why would we listen to him? His stated objective is to "make us miserable like unto himself" (see 2 Nephi 2:18, 27). How is he [the devil]? He is single, he is the father of lies, and will eventually be cast out forever from the presence of God. Everything that has Satan's fingerprints on it will lead us in that direction.

"Ye endeavored to believe that ye should receive the blessing which was offered unto you; but behold, verily I say unto you there were fears in your hearts, and verily this is the reason that ye did not receive" (D&C 67:3). He asked: "You mean, fear blocks answers to prayers?" It certainly does according to what the Lord has revealed. Then one final scripture. "Look unto me in every thought; doubt not, fear not" (D&C 6:36). In one short verse the Lord informs us that He doesn't use doubt or fear.

As I looked at him, he seemed rather uncomfortable. He asked if we could postpone the recommend interview until the next day, to which I agreed. The following day I heard a knock on my door and I invited whoever was there to come in. My ward member opened the door and stuck his head in with a big smile on his face. Rather insensitively I asked: "Oh, did you find number five?" To which he laughingly replied: "No, but I did find number four!" He asked if his fiancé could come in with him and chat for a minute? I responded in the positive. A beautiful young lady came in sporting an engagement ring. He said: "Bishop, how did you know that I didn't receive a negative answer?" I said: "Because you had what you considered to be a 'stupor of thought' but your heart was not turned away from her." Then I reminded him that either he or the adversary could duplicate one domain (heart or mind) but neither he nor the adversary could duplicate them both at the same time or that would negate the spirit of revelation.

Happily the temple recommend interview became their

pre-marriage interview. I wonder how many times people have mistakenly made a decision because they failed to realize that when only half a formula is applied to a problem, almost always the answer is wrong?

As you prepare for your mission and life, practice learning to recognize and respond to Divine answers to your prayers. Then you can lead others to Christ by teaching them what you have practiced and perfected in your own life.

*Chapter 19*

# TEACHING BY
# THE SPIRIT

"And the Spirit shall be given unto you by the prayer of faith; and if ye receive not the Spirit ye shall not teach" (D&C 42:14). So important is learning to teach by the Spirit that the Lord states that without the Spirit you might instruct, entertain, take up time, or anything else, but teaching (which causes people to change their lives) can only be accomplished when the Spirit is present.

So how does one get the Spirit so he or she can teach? The Lord already answered that in the opening scripture: "the Spirit shall be given unto you by the prayer of faith." What is the difference between "prayer" and the "prayer of faith?" Faith! If you pray believing that the Spirit will confirm what you are teaching, and you are sincere, and you are teaching true doctrine, then the Spirit will confirm your words to your investigators.

Nephi had struggled over many years to teach his brothers and his people. At the end of his long prophetic career he taught:

And now I, Nephi, cannot write all the things which were taught among my people; neither am I

mighty in writing, like unto speaking; for **when a man
speaketh by the power of the Holy Ghost the power
of the Holy Ghost carrieth it unto the hearts of the
children of men.** (2 Nephi 33:1, emphasis added)

Your job is not to "convert" people — it is to teach them
with such power and clarity that they cannot misunder-
stand the gospel. Then the Holy Ghost will carry the
message "unto" their hearts — not "into." The investigators
must make a conscious effort to either open their hearts to
the message taught by you but delivered and testified to by
the Holy Ghost, or harden their hearts against the message.
The Lord taught: "Behold, here is the agency of man, and
here is the condemnation of man; because that which was
from the beginning is plainly manifest unto them, and they
receive not the light" (D&C 93:31).

Too often young, enthusiastic missionaries want to
convert people by their own personality and charisma.
That was never the Lord's program. In fact he described His
messengers in the latter-days by saying:

> Wherefore, I call upon the weak things of the
> world, those who are unlearned and despised, to
> thrash the nations by the power of my Spirit;
>
> And their arm shall be my arm, and I will be their
> shield and their buckler; and I will gird up their
> loins, and they shall fight manfully for me; and their
> enemies shall be under their feet; and I will let fall
> the sword in their behalf, and by the fire of mine
> indignation will I preserve them. (D&C 35:13-14)

Why would the Lord send missionaries who are "weak,
unlearned, and despised" to represent Him? He answered:
"to thrash the nations by the power of my Spirit." Yes, you
should use all the intellectual power you possess. You
should develop people-skills, including manners, charisma, and personality. But those attributes will only
enhance you as a missionary — they will not enable you to

be successful without the power of the Spirit. The Savior taught a truth essential to successful gospel leadership when He said: "I am the vine, ye are the branches: He that abideth in me, and I in him, the same bringeth forth much fruit: **for without me ye can do nothing**" (John 15:5, emphasis added).

So what is the role of the Spirit? "For my Spirit is sent forth into the world to enlighten the humble and contrite, and to the condemnation of the ungodly" (D&C 136:33). As we will discuss in future chapters, we were all taught the gospel in the pre-earth life by Celestial Teachers. "But the Comforter, which is the Holy Ghost, whom the Father will send in my name, he shall teach you all things, and **bring all things to your remembrance**, whatsoever I have said unto you" (John 14:26, emphasis added). So the Holy Ghost is the medium through which the veil, which was placed over our minds so we could learn to live by faith, is thinned to where the sincere investigator can "remember" what they learned in the pre-earth life. Therefore, you are not teaching them anything new, you are reminding them of what they understood and accepted before ever coming to this earth. Perhaps that is why the Lord said: "And ye are called to bring to pass the gathering of mine elect; for mine elect hear my voice and harden not their hearts" (D&C 29:7).

If you can grasp the magnitude of the trust that Heavenly Father has placed in you as His mouthpiece to the people of the world, you will realize that a mission is not a time to play or goof around. You become the voice of God to the people you teach.

> What I the Lord have spoken, I have spoken, and I excuse not myself; and though the heavens and the earth pass away, my word shall not pass away, but shall all be fulfilled, **whether by mine own voice or by the voice of my servants, it is the same.** (D&C 1:38, emphasis added)

How can you possibly teach as God does when you are so young an inexperienced?

Again I say, hearken ye elders of my church, whom I have appointed: Ye are not sent forth to be taught, but to teach the children of men the things which I have put into your hands by the power of my Spirit;

And **ye are to be taught from on high**. Sanctify yourselves and ye shall be endowed with power, that ye may give even as I have spoken. (D&C 43:15-16, emphasis added)

Think of it! You are to be taught by revelation what and how to teach the people of the world. And when you effectively perform your duty, you will stand as judges against those who reject your testimony in the day of judgment.

And in whatsoever house ye enter, and they receive you, leave your blessing upon that house.

And in whatsoever house ye enter, and they receive you not, ye shall depart speedily from that house, and shake off the dust of your feet as a testimony against them.

And you shall be filled with joy and gladness; and know this, that in the day of judgment you shall be judges of that house, and condemn them;

And it shall be more tolerable for the heathen in the day of judgment, than for that house; therefore, gird up your loins and be faithful, and ye shall overcome all things, and be lifted up at the last day. Even so. Amen. (D&C 75:19-22)

I realize this has been a lot of scriptures to read, but without the basic understanding of what the Lord has revealed, you will be less than effective in teaching. How do you learn all of the thousands of passages necessary to have an understanding of the gospel? The key is revealed by the

Lord: "Neither take ye thought beforehand what ye shall say; but **treasure up in your minds continually the words of life**, and it shall be given you in the very hour that portion that shall be meted unto every man" (D&C 84:85, emphasis added, see also D&C 100:5-8).

As obvious as the need to study scripture seems, too many missionaries take a very casual approach. Unless you religiously adhere to the rules in the white handbook about personal and companion study, it is easy to fill your time with other things. The price you must pay to become a gospel scholar has no shortcuts. Start immediately, if you haven't already, disciplining yourself to study every single day. Ask yourself questions like: "What question would someone have to ask so that this passage of scripture would be the answer?" Search for ways to apply the gospel, as taught in the scriptures, in your everyday life. Learn to recognize the impact that the gospel has in your life. You might ask yourself: "If someone could reach in and remove the gospel and its influence entirely from my life, what difference would it make?" You will discover that the gospel impacts every single aspect of your life, from the way you treat your family and friends to the way you handle crises and problems. It gives you direction in your life and helps you avoid the pitfalls placed in your way by the adversary. I suspect your life wouldn't even be an empty shell of what you are now if the gospel were removed.

In the mission field you will learn to discover which part of the gospel will satisfy the needs of your investigators. It will be different for each investigator. One may have suffered the loss of a loved one, another may be having marital or family problems, another may have experienced a financial setback, still another may be struggling with wanting to continue the battle of life and is thinking of "ending it all." Everyone on earth has a need that the gospel can meet. Your job is to know the gospel well enough to teach the part that fills that need.

As you teach, the Lord has given three keys to recognize that you are teaching by the Spirit.

> Therefore, why is it that ye cannot understand and know, that he that receiveth the word by the Spirit of truth receiveth it as it is preached by the Spirit of truth?
>
> Wherefore, he that preacheth and he that receiveth, [1] understand one another, and [2] both are edified and [3] rejoice together.
>
> And that which doth not edify is not of God, and is darkness. (D&C 50:21-23)

As you teach, watch for verbal or visual cues to determine whether the people you are teaching understand what you are teaching. You might ask questions to allow them opportunities to verbalize what you have taught. If they have a confused look on their faces or seem to be losing interest, then you can be assured that (a) you are not teaching by the Spirit, (b) they are not listening by the Spirit, or (c) both of the above. You are wasting your time, the Lord's time and the people's time when trying to teach without the Spirit present.

Paul taught:

> For what man knoweth the things of a man, save the spirit of man which is in him? even so the things of God knoweth no man, but the Spirit of God.
>
> But the natural man receiveth not the things of the Spirit of God: for they are foolishness unto him: **neither can he know them**, because they are spiritually discerned. (1 Corinthians 2:11,14, emphasis added)

It isn't that people don't want to know or that they lack the intelligence to understand. Without the Spirit they

**cannot** understand. Therefore, if you can't get the Spirit during a discussion, it is best to leave and set another time to teach.

In order to qualify for the Spirit, you must be a clean and worthy vessel. If you have sins of which you have not repented, or if you are not obeying mission rules, then you'll not qualify for the strength of the Spirit you need to lead others to Christ. If you and your companion are clean and worthy, then the Lord will guide you to those whom He has prepared to accept the gospel. Your teaching by the power of the Spirit is just the catalyst to allow the Spirit to convince the investigator of the truthfulness of the gospel.

Since the chapter began with the Lord's instruction on how to get the Spirit (by the prayer of faith), it would be worthwhile to reemphasize the vital role that prayer plays. Whether you are teaching a discussion, giving a talk in church, talking to someone on the street, or any other activity where the gospel is being presented, you should get into the habit of pausing, praying for the Spirit, and then listening to the promptings of the Spirit as you proceed. With the Spirit accompanying your teaching, people will understand your language easier, they will identify with the principles you are teaching, their hearts will be touched, and those who are prepared will join the Church.

Teaching with the Spirit will make the difference between a successful, enjoyable mission and just being away from home for a year and a half or two years. Do what is necessary to learn to recognize what the Spirit feels like to you. The Spirit may have a different effect on each individual. Some may feel a warm, tingling sensation in their chests. Others may find that their minds work a thousand miles an hour. Still others may experience an excited, hyper state. Yet others may feel a calm, soothing feeling. Don't try to tell people what they will feel like when the Spirit is with them. However, when you feel the Spirit with you, it is helpful to ask the investigator what they are feeling and then associate whatever feeling they describe with the Spirit.

Once you have taught with the Spirit, you will never again be satisfied teaching on your own. When you speak by the power of the Spirit, you are literally acting as the angels in heaven do. Nephi explained:

> Do ye not remember that I said unto you that after ye had received the Holy Ghost ye could speak with the tongue of angels? And now, how could ye speak with the tongue of angels save it were by the Holy Ghost?
>
> Angels speak by the power of the Holy Ghost; wherefore, they speak the words of Christ. Wherefore, I said unto you, feast upon the words of Christ; for behold, the words of Christ will tell you all things what ye should do. (2 Nephi 32:2-3)

You can't start too early to learn to recognize and teach by the power of the Spirit. You won't learn how to teach overnight or even during your stay in the MTC. You must practice constantly and little by little the Lord will increase your understanding and you'll begin to develop power in your teaching. Now is the hour to begin. Don't delay.

*Chapter 20*

# THE PLAN OF SALVATION –
# THE PRE-EARTH LIFE

Joseph Smith once taught:

> In the first place, I wish to go back to the beginning — to the morn of creation. There is the starting point for us to look to, in order to understand and be fully acquainted with the mind, purposes and decrees of the Great Elohim, who sits in yonder heavens as he did at the creation of this world. It is necessary for us to have an understanding of God himself in the beginning. If we start right, it is easy to go right all the time; but if we start wrong, we may go wrong, and it be a hard matter to get right. (*Teachings of the Prophet Joseph Smith*, p.343)

The world in which you live and will serve your mission has lost its direction. Now, instead of recognizing that God is our Father and we are His children, we have devolved into believing that we got our start through evolutionary actions millions of years ago. Unless people know who they are, why they are here, and where they are going after death, they have very little incentive to live the way God requires.

For this and the next three chapters, we will review some of the basics concerning the plan of salvation. It wouldn't be wise or possible to write all we know concerning this great subject. But if you get the big picture, everything you have been taught for years in church classes will make perfect sense.

In order to see who you really are, answer the following questions: if we stripped away your mortal body, which the scriptures inform us was created in the image of God, what is left? The answer: your spirit body. Is it male or female? According to what is taught in "The Family — a Proclamation to the World" issued by the First Presidency and the Twelve Apostles in 1995, the gender you are now you had in the pre-earth life. How did you get your mortal body? By the power of procreation exercised by your father and mother. What did your spirit body look like? At least to a degree, it looked like your physical body looks. It also appeared to be solid like your physical body. But if you tried to touch another person's spirit body with your physical body, what would you feel? The answer: nothing. The gross elements which made up our physical body cannot feel the fine elements which make up a spirit body. Can a spirit body touch another spirit body? And if so, what will they feel? Parley P. Pratt taught that the spirit bodies are just as tangible to each other as our physical bodies are to each other (see *Key to the Science of Theology*, p.130).

If we strip away our spirit bodies, what is left? Only intelligence or spirits. Are they male or female? We don't know, it hasn't yet been revealed. Do they have shape like we do? We don't know, it hasn't yet been revealed. Where did they come from? They are co-eternal with God, they have always existed. So the "you" that is really you was not created or made but has existed forever (see D&C 93:29).

How did we get our spirit body? We have the same relationship to God our Father that we have to our earthly father and mother. Through the proper and eternal use of the procreative powers, our Heavenly Parents provided spirit bodies for Their spirit children.

The scriptures refer to our pre-earth life as "in the beginning or before the world was" (D&C 93:7). Though in the broadest sense, we had no beginning — we have existed forever, from a more limited perspective, we had our beginning when we received our spirit bodies from God.

From our very beginning, we wanted to progress and eventually become like our Heavenly Father. Joseph Smith taught:

> The first principles of man are self-existent with God. God himself, finding he was in the midst of spirits and glory, because he was more intelligent, saw proper to institute laws whereby the rest could have a privilege to advance like himself. The relationship we have with God places us in a situation to advance in knowledge. He has power to institute laws to instruct the weaker intelligences, that they may be exalted with himself, so that they might have one glory upon another, and all that knowledge, power, glory, and intelligence, which is requisite in order to save them in the world of spirits. (*Teachings of the Prophet Joseph Smith*, p.354)

The laws became the stepping stones to help us advance to become like God. However, God refused to force His spirit children to accept His plan or obey His commandments. He gave each son and daughter agency. With that freedom to choose came accountability for the consequences of our choices. Some of the sons and daughters of God were diligent in obeying those laws, which Elder Bruce R. McConkie called "the gospel of God," in the pre-earth life. "The Messiah thus becomes the One through whom salvation comes. The gospel of God, which is the plan of salvation, becomes his gospel" (*The Promised*

*Messiah*, p. 67). Understanding that the gospel of God in the pre-earth life is the same as the gospel of Jesus Christ in mortality, then you are really not teaching people something they didn't know but reminding them of something they were taught by Celestial Teachers, understood, and lived with some degree of valiancy for many, many years before their mortal birth.

God revealed to Abraham:

> Now the Lord had shown unto me, Abraham, the intelligences that were organized before the world was; and among all these there were many of the noble and great ones;
>
> And God saw these souls that they were good, and he stood in the midst of them, and he said: These I will make my rulers; for he stood among those that were spirits, and he saw that they were good; and he said unto me: Abraham, thou art one of them; thou wast chosen before thou wast born. (Abraham 3:22-23)

Note the following doctrinal issues which are clarified in the above passage:

- Some spirit children were noble and great which suggests that some were "not so noble and not so great." Some members of the church have suggested that only those who were called as apostles and prophets were among the noble and great ones. Neither the scriptures nor the latter-day prophets agree. The Prophet Joseph Smith taught: "Every man who has a calling to minister to the inhabitants of the world was ordained to that very purpose in the Grand Council of heaven before this world was" (*Teachings of the Prophet Joseph Smith*, p. 365). Considering the entire history of humankind, it is ludicrous to believe that those who are members of the Church and called to serve were not part of the group labeled as noble and great.

- God declared that these souls were good. A soul (see D&C 88:15) is defined as a body and a spirit combined. Therefore, it appears that God is seeing us in mortality and in our resurrected state. That wouldn't be difficult for Him since everything, past, present, and future are to Him one eternal "now" (see *Teachings of the Prophet Joseph Smith*, p. 220). He who never lies and never makes a mistake said we were good. Perhaps it would be wise not to argue with God, accept what He said of us, and spend our time acting the part and fulfilling our foreordination.

- Certain of the noble and great ones were foreordained to leadership positions in the councils in heaven. Joseph Smith said: "I believe that every person who is called to do an important work in the kingdom of God, was called to that work and foreordained to that work before the world was." Then he added this: "I believe that I was foreordained to the work that I am called to do" (*Documentary History of the Church*, 6:364).

God continued His vision to Abraham:

> And there stood one among them that was like unto God, and he said unto those who were with him: We will go down, for there is space there, and we will take of these materials, and we will make an earth whereon these may dwell;
>
> And we will prove them herewith, to see if they will do all things whatsoever the Lord their God shall command them. (Abraham 3:24-25)

Since the entirety of our Father's plan was to help us gain experiences to become like Him, it would seem reasonable that those who had achieved the status of "noble and great" would be allowed to gain further experience by helping to create the earth. Without any interpretation, that is exactly what Abraham saw (as recorded in verse 24).

There is even a further reason for expanding our understanding about the creation and the part we played. First, we must have known considerably more before coming here than we now know. Joseph F. Smith taught:

> Can we know anything here that we did not know before we came? Are not the means of knowledge in the first estate equal to those of this? I think that the spirit, before and after this probation, possesses greater facilities, aye, manifold greater, for the acquisition of knowledge, than while manacled and shut up in the prison-house of mortality. ( *Gospel Doctrine*, p. 13)

Second, since we helped to create the physical earth on which we live, why would we suspect God would place us on earth without our being able to "create" our own social world, intellectual world, physical surroundings world, or emotional world? When we view ourselves as helpless animals subject to the conditions into which we were born, we fail to see earth life as another step in our learning to become like our Heavenly Father. Is He a creator? Then we can be too. Is He in control of Himself and His world? Then we can be too.

Third, mortality was designed to be a proving grounds. We would be tested in "all things" to see if we would be obedient. Then which part of our mortal experience do we expect will not be subject to satanic testing? We don't need to go looking for the testing — it will find us.

Too many Latter-day Saints seem to believe that if we are living the gospel, nothing bad should happen to us. If that were the case, the Savior would have had a trouble-free life. Since He was tested in every temptation common to man (see Hebrews 4:15), then why should we expect less from our mortal testing?

Perhaps Abraham 3:26 is the most revelatory verse in all scripture concerning how to be eternally successful.

And they who keep their first estate shall be added upon; and they who keep not their first estate shall not have glory in the same kingdom with those who keep their first estate; and they who keep their second estate shall have glory added upon their heads for ever and ever.

Our "first estate" was our pre-earth life. We kept it by voluntarily bringing our spirit bodies into subjection to Christ, Who was the Champion of God's Plan of Happiness for His children. When Lucifer, a son of the morning, learned that mortality would constitute the final great test preceding exaltation, and that it would involve a veil of forgetfulness being placed over our minds, and that some would fail to qualify for eternal life, he rebelled. His proposed implementation of the Father's plan was that the "cause and effect" relationship of actions to consequences be done away with. We could do whatever we wanted without fear of any punishment, and exaltation would still be given to all (see Bruce R. McConkie, *The Millennial Messiah*, pp. 666-667).

At times I have heard teachers in the Church promote the doctrine that the devil's plan was to force us to be good. When has Satan ever forced anyone to be good? His objective, which is openly taught in today's world, was freedom to act however we wanted to without any accountability for our actions.

Lucifer must have taunted those who were less noble and had not been as valiant in keeping the rules of the gospel of God in the pre-earth life. In my mind I can hear him saying: "You weren't successful in living God's laws while in His very presence. What makes you think you could succeed if this veil of forgetfulness was placed over your mind?" So appealing was his logic that one-third part of the hosts of heaven followed him (see Revelation 12:4-9 and Moses 4:1-4).

The reward for keeping our first estate was that we would "be added upon." The prophets have informed us that that phrase means getting a physical body. Those who didn't keep their first estate (Satan and one third part of the hosts of heaven) were deprived of ever having a physical body. Joseph Smith taught:

> We came to this earth that we might have a body and present it pure before God in the celestial kingdom. The great principle of happiness consists in having a body. The devil has no body, and herein is his punishment. He is pleased when he can obtain the tabernacle of man, and when cast out by the Savior he asked to go into the herd of swine, showing that he would prefer a swine's body to having none. (*Teachings of the Prophet Joseph Smith,* p.181)

However, Abraham didn't say the devil and his followers wouldn't receive a body. He said they wouldn't "have glory" in the same kingdom as those who were obedient. Here the body is equated with glory. Now the second half of verse 26 makes much more sense: "and they who keep their second estate shall have glory added upon their heads for ever and ever." If we kept our first estate by voluntarily bringing our spirit bodies in subjection to Christ, how do we keep our second estate? Just as our first estate was our spirit bodies, our second estate is our physical bodies. Following the same logic, we keep our second estate by bringing our physical bodies in subjection to our spirit bodies, which are already subject to Christ.

So the battleground is set for mortality: our celestial spirit bodies warring against our unruly, telestial, physical bodies. The physical body always wanting to do whatever feels good, whatever it wants to do, or whatever is contrary to the commandments of God, and our eternal spirit trying to bring it under control.

Since our sole objective was to become like God, and since we call God "our Heavenly Father," and since He became a Father by exercising His procreative powers, what would you conclude would be one of the most challenging tests of mortality? Wouldn't it be the using and not abusing of our procreative powers? If we abuse the sexual powers God has temporarily loaned to us, then we shouldn't be too surprised if they are not restored to our resurrected bodies. That is exactly what the gospel teaches. The only ones who have the power to continue having children in the life to come are those who are exalted (see D&C 131:1-4). Everyone else will live "separately and singly in their saved condition to all eternity" (see D&C 132:15-17).

So those who keep their second estate — control their bodies and procreative powers, will have "glory," or the power to have children eternally, added to them forever and ever. Now we are ready to look more closely at mortality. For one final look back, remember that God doesn't do anything without purpose. Therefore all the experiences we had in pre-earth life and those we are going through here in mortality are all calculated to help us learn, grow, and progress to become like our Heavenly Father. Because of the veil of forgetfulness, we seldom see the big picture which, when seen again, will make sense of all the senseless things that happen to us.

Earth life, then, does not constitute the beginning of the test of godhood. It must be almost viewed as the final exam. Much of the talent, personality, and inclination towards spirituality had already been developed before we were ever born. Our mortal life here on earth is not the first time we exercised our agency. Now is the time to see whether we have truly internalized the principles of godliness.

You cannot afford to go into the mission field without

having the vision of what life is all about. Where did we come from? Why are we here? And how do we pass the test of mortality? which is the subject of the next chapter.

*Chapter 21*

# The Plan of Salvation – Mortality – How to Pass the Test

We have just completed a chapter on the doctrine explaining our pre-earth life which sets the Church apart from the rest of the world. Now we'll turn our attention to the time between our mortal birth and physical death. An understanding of why we are here and how we can tell whether we are passing the test of mortality, even though plainly taught in scriptures and by modern prophets, seems to have escaped many Latter-day Saints, and is virtually unknown to the people of the world.

Keep in mind that God is our personal and loving Father. We know Him better than we know our earthly fathers. Brigham Young taught:

> I want to tell you, each and every one of you, that you are well acquainted with God our Heavenly Father, or the great Elohim. You are all well acquainted with him, for there is not a soul of you but what has lived in his house and dwelt with him year after year; and yet you are seeking to become

acquainted with him, when the fact is, you have merely forgotten what you did know.

There is not a person here today but what is a son or a daughter of that Being. In the spirit world their spirits were first begotten and brought forth, and they lived there with their parents for ages before they came here. This, perhaps, is hard for many to believe, but it is the greatest nonsense in the world not to believe it. If you do not believe it, cease to call him Father; and when you pray, pray to some other character. (*Discourses of Brigham Young*, p.50)

God knew and determined where, when, and how long each person would live on earth. "And hath made of one blood all nations of men for to dwell on all the face of the earth, and **hath determined the times before appointed, and the bounds of their habitation**" (Acts 17:26, emphasis added). The Lord revealed to Moses: "When the most High divided to the nations their inheritance, when he separated the sons of Adam, he set the bounds of the people according to the number of the children of Israel" (Deuteronomy 32:8). So each person on earth was assigned a time and a place to play their part in the great drama of life.

It is most important to understand that God knows the end from the beginning (see Isaiah 46:10). We are not here to prove our willingness to obey God — He already knows the end. We are here to prove to ourselves that we can be trusted to obey even when our memory of the spiritual past has been temporarily taken from us.

It is also essential that you know that this earth life represents just a small (but very important) fraction of our entire existence. A sufficient portion of the test of godhood was passed before coming here that people who are not permitted to enjoy a lengthy stay on the earth (little children who die before the age of accountability) automatically qualify for the celestial kingdom. The scriptures teach: "And little children also have eternal life" (Mosiah 15:25). This same doctrine was shown to the Prophet Joseph Smith in a vision. "And I also beheld that all children who die before they arrive at the years of accountability are saved in the celestial kingdom of heaven" (D&C 137:10).

Although we would love to see all of our children live lengthy lives, the knowledge that all little children are saved in the celestial kingdom is a doctrine that gives hope and comfort to grieving parents who lose a child to death. You will use this doctrine, which differs dramatically from what most other churches teach, in many different settings. Make sure you understand it well.

How do we, who have lived to maturity, pass the test of mortality? You will remember the chapter which described the eight points of "My Gospel." The gospel is the vehicle which enables mankind to travel through life with happiness rather than misery and sorrow. Knowing and living the gospel doesn't mean there won't be trials and temptations, sickness and set-backs, or disappointments and diseases. It helps put everything into eternal perspective, where those things which seem to be without meaning become understandable and endurable without our becoming angry at God.

Now let's specifically answer the question of how we know we are passing the test of mortality. Think about the work that is done for the dead in our temples. Do we have primary, Young Men and Young Women's, or Relief Society there? No! All that is done in the temples is the bare minimum necessary for those who did not have the chance on earth, to gain the opportunity to achieve eternal life in the celestial kingdom by accepting ordinances vicariously performed.

So if we can determine what we do in the temples, we

can know what the bare necessities are to gain eternal life. First, there is baptism for the dead. Second, those baptized for the dead are confirmed on behalf of the person for whom they are acting as proxy. Third, priesthood is bestowed on behalf of deceased men. Fourth, the temple endowment is administered on behalf of the deceased. Fifth, couples are married and sealed by proxy and their children are sealed to them. That is all!

A person can easily tell whether they are passing the test of life if they are, at the proper time, making sacred covenants and entering into sacred ordinances. If, through no fault of their own, a person is interrupted in their quest to have all the ordinances performed for them (e.g. they die), then they will not be denied eternal blessings because others will be permitted to act as proxy for them. So if you were to die while serving your mission (being single), you would find your eternal companion in the Spirit World, appear to someone in the temple during the early days of the Millennium, they would perform the marriage for you, and you two would continue on to eternal life.

What if a person lied to be baptized or to gain entrance to the temple for those sacred ordinances? The Lord has a safety valve so that no unworthy person can receive an eternal blessing. To the Prophet Joseph Smith the Lord revealed:

> And verily I say unto you, that the conditions of this law are these: All covenants...that are not [1] made and [2] entered into and [3] sealed by the Holy Spirit of promise, ...are of no efficacy, virtue, or force in and after the resurrection from the dead; for all contracts that are not made unto this end have an end when men are dead. (D&C 132:7)

We "make" the covenants by doing what the Lord has prescribed. For example we go into the water and are immersed in order to comply with the Lord's requirement for baptism, because He so commanded it. When Adam questioned the Lord as to why man must repent and be baptized, the Lord explained, "For **by the water ye keep the commandment**; by the Spirit ye are justified, and by the blood ye are sanctified" (Moses 6:60, emphasis added). We make the covenant of marriage by kneeling at the altar of a temple and saying "yes" at the appropriate time.

We "enter into" the covenants by daily living the requirements associated with the covenant. In baptism, for instance, we commit that we will "mourn with those that mourn; yea, and comfort those that stand in need of comfort, and to stand as witnesses of God at all times and in all things, and in all places that ye may be in, even until death" (Mosiah 18:9). As long as we do our best to keep our part of the covenant, the Lord will fulfill His promises. If we fail to continue to "enter into" the covenant (in other words, we stop living what we committed to do), then the promised blessings will not come to us. The Lord revealed:

Who am I, saith the Lord, that have promised and have not fulfilled?

I command and men obey not; I revoke and they receive not the blessing.

Then they say in their hearts: This is not the work of the Lord, for his promises are not fulfilled. But wo unto such, for their reward lurketh beneath, and not from above. (D&C 58:31-33)

As long as we continue to enter into our covenants by living them, the covenant is "sealed by the Holy Spirit of Promise." That means that the Holy Spirit is signifying by His presence that, if we continue faithful, the promised blessing will be sealed upon us. So how can we tell whether we are living as well as the Lord expects us to live? He said: "And the place where it is my will that you should tarry, for the main, shall be signalized unto you by the peace and power of my Spirit, that shall flow unto you" (D&C 111:8).

You can tell 24/7 whether you are doing an acceptable job in keeping the covenants you have made by the presence or absence of the Spirit. Remember what the Lord told Adam "by the Spirit ye are justified" (Moses 6:60). When the Spirit is with you, you are just or justified before God, which means you are not condemned or viewed as guilty. Heavenly Father signalizes His Divine disapproval by partially withdrawing His Spirit.

If you can live your life so that the Spirit is your constant companion, then you have no need to fear. Whenever you die (with the Spirit of the Lord) you will be allowed to progress until you make the highest degree of the celestial kingdom. Brigham Young taught:

> It is present salvation and the present influence of the Holy Ghost that we need every day to keep us on saving ground. When an individual refuses to comply with the further requirements of Heaven, then the sins he had formerly committed return upon his head; his former righteousness departs from him, and is not accounted to him for righteousness; but if he had continued in righteousness and obedience to the requirements of Heaven, he is saved all the time, through baptism, the laying on of hands, and obeying the commandments of the Lord and all that is required of him by the heavens— the living oracles. He is saved now, next week, next year, and continually, and is prepared for the celestial kingdom of God whenever the times comes for him to inherit it. (*Journal of Discourses* 8:124)

Too many Latter-day Saints worry without cause because they have not yet achieved perfection. If you can teach them to recognize when God is manifesting to them that they are justified, you can assist in lowering the level of concern. So in a nutshell: as long as I feel the presence of the Spirit, I am living as well as the Lord expects me to live, given the amount of light and knowledge He has revealed to me. And if I continue, I will receive exaltation in His kingdom.

It is frustrating to see our goal of perfection and yet fall short because we are mortals. Elder Neal A. Maxwell said:

Now may I speak, not to the slacker in the Kingdom, but to those who carry their own load and more; not to those lulled into false security, but to those buffeted by false insecurity, who, though laboring devotedly in the Kingdom, have recurring feelings of falling forever short.[...]

The first thing to be said of this feeling of inadequacy is that it is normal. There is no way the Church can honestly describe where we must yet go and what we must yet do without creating a sense of immense distance. Following celestial road signs while in telestial traffic jams is not easy, especially when we are not just moving next door — or even across town.

In a Kingdom where perfection is an eventual expectation, each other's needs for improvement have a way of being noticed.[...]

Some of us who would not chastise a neighbor for his frailties have a field day with our own. Some of us stand before no more harsh a judge than ourselves, a judge who stubbornly refuses to admit much happy evidence and who cares nothing for due process. Fortunately, the Lord loves us more than we love ourselves.[...]

Yes, brothers and sisters, this is a gospel of grand expectations, but God's grace is sufficient for each of us. Discouragement is not the absence of adequacy but the absence of courage, and our personal progress should be yet another way we witness to the wonder of it all!

True, there are no instant Christians, but there are constant Christians! (*Conference Report* Oct. 1976, pp. 14-16)

If you, your companion, or any member thinks perfection is attainable in this life, you should read what the Prophet Joseph Smith taught:

When you climb up a ladder, you must begin at the bottom, and ascend step by step, until you arrive at the top; and so it is with the principles of the Gospel — you must begin with the first, and go on until you learn all the principles of exaltation. But it will be a great while after you have passed through the veil before you will have learned them. It is not all to be comprehended in this world; it will be a great work to learn our salvation and exaltation even beyond the grave. (*Teachings of the Prophet Joseph Smith*, p. 348)

Perhaps one final quote before closing the chapter on mortality. Elder Bruce R. McConkie said:

I'd like to append to them the fact — and this is a true gospel verity — that everyone in the Church who is on the straight and narrow path, who is striving and struggling and desiring to do what is right, though far from perfect in this life; if he passes out of this life while he's on the straight and narrow, he's going to go on to an eternal reward in his Father's kingdom.

You don't need to get a complex or get a feeling that you have to be perfect to be saved. You don't. There's only been one perfect person, and that's the Lord Jesus, but in order to be saved on the straight and narrow path — thus charting a course leading to eternal life — and then, being on that path, pass out of this life in full fellowship. I'm not saying that you don't have to keep the commandments. I'm saying you don't have to be perfect to be saved. The way it operates is this: You get on the path that's named the 'straight and narrow.' You do it by entering the gate of repentance and baptism. The straight and narrow path leads from the gate of repentance and baptism, a very great distance, to a reward that's called eternal life. If you're on that path and pressing forward, and you die, you'll never get off the path. There is no such thing as falling off the straight and narrow path in the life to come, and the reason is that this life is the time that is given to men to prepare for eternity. Now is the time and the day of your salvation, so if you're working zealously in this life — though you haven't fully overcome the world and you haven't done all you hoped you might do — you're still going to be saved. You don't have to do what Jacob said, "Go beyond the mark." You don't have to live a life that's truer than true. You don't have to have an excessive zeal that becomes fanatical and unbalancing. What you have to do is stay in the mainstream of the Church and live as upright and decent people in the Church    keeping the commandments, paying your tithing, serving in the organizations of the Church, loving the Lord, staying on the straight and narrow path. If you're on that path when death comes — because this is the time and day appointed, this is the probationary estate — you'll never fall off from it, and for all practical purposes, your calling and election is made sure. ("The Probationary Test of Mortality," address given at the University of Utah, January 10, 1982, p. 11)

Don't lose hope. Although we live in a world that is rapidly self-destructing, we were not sent here to fail. You are sent to hold up the light of the Savior to the world. If you will live your testimony then your light will so shine that people will see the impact that the gospel has in your life and want to know what sets you apart from everyone else. When you fall short of perfection, don't get down on yourself. Just repent and get back on the straight and narrow path and let the Lord heal your soul. By enduring to the end one day at a time, you will find that mortality, although a test, can be enjoyable and doable. Don't make exaltation so difficult for members and investigators that only a select few are able to attain it. You will need to strike a balance between trying to make eternal life too easy (nothing required) and too difficult. With the help of the Spirit you will not fail. Help people find hope in a hopeless world.

*Chapter 22*

# THE PLAN OF SALVATION –
# DEATH AND THE SPIRIT WORLD

One of the universal experiences that all mankind must face, but few understand, is death. When an elderly person or one who has suffered for a prolonged period dies, even those who have no concept of an afterlife view death as a blessing. However, Jacob taught,

> For as **death hath passed upon all men, to fulfil the merciful plan of the great Creator**, there must needs be a power of resurrection, and the resurrection must needs come unto man by reason of the fall; and the fall came by reason of transgression; and because man became fallen they were cut off from the presence of the Lord. (2 Nephi 9:6, emphasis added)

Jacob didn't differentiate between the old and the young dying. In some way that we must understand, death is another vital step in fulfilling the plan of the great Creator.

How can death be a merciful act when it is a child who dies or a young person who is killed in a tragic accident? The Prophet Joseph Smith taught, "The only difference between the old and young dying is, one lives longer in heaven and eternal light and glory than the other, and is freed a little sooner from this miserable wicked world (*Documentary History of the Church* 4:554). That is just backwards from the way most people view early death.

Says one: "I know the person is better off dead, but the way they died was horrible." Another prophet, John Taylor, stated: "God, in his eternal decrees, has ordained that all men must die, but as to the mode and manner of our exit, it matters very little" (*Journal of Discourses* 17:131).

There must be something about death and dying that the prophets understand, which many of us do not, that causes them to view the dying process as a kind of graduation into a better life. As we consider the death process and what little has been revealed about the post-mortal spirit world, try to see as the prophets do. Then, as you teach the people of the world, whether they are currently members of the church or not, you will be able to bring peace, hope, and comfort to those who are grieving. Brigham Young taught:

> We shall turn round and look upon it (the valley of death) and think, when we have crossed it, why this is the greatest advantage of my whole existence, for I have passed from a state of sorrow, grief, mourning, woe, misery, pain, anguish and disap-pointment into a state of existence where I can enjoy life to the fullest extent as far as that can be done without a body. My spirit is set free, I thirst no more, I want to sleep no more, I hunger no more, I tire no more, I run, I walk, I labor, I go, I come, I do this, I do that, whatever is required of me, nothing like pain or weariness, I am full of life, full of vigor, and I enjoy the presence of my Heavenly Father. (*Journal of Discourses* 17:142)

The freedom that will be enjoyed in the spirit world by

those who have faithfully passed the tests of mortality outweighs the happiness and joys of mortality. God has determined that when our mortal bodies become unfit to house our eternal spirits, through sickness, accident, or old age, then death is the merciful release provided to enable our spirits to continue progressing. President George Albert Smith said:

It would be tragic if a man, when he grew to be old were compelled to remain distressed and helpless in mortality, continuing on and on without the ability to enjoy longer life here. And so the Lord has decreed that we all come into the world in the same way, our time here being limited. We all have an opportunity to enjoy happiness in mortality, and then, if we have been wise, we pass on, prepared for eternal happiness in the celestial kingdom when this earth shall be cleansed and purified by fire and will be presided over by our Heavenly Father and by our Elder Brother, Jesus Christ, as one of their dominions. With that assurance in our lives, death is not such a serious matter. (*Improvement Era*, June 1945)

Where is the Spirit World where the spirits of all mankind go when they die? It is right here on earth, but in a dimension which our mortal eyes cannot see. Brigham Young stated:

Is the spirit world here? It is not beyond the sun, but is on this earth that was organized for the people that have lived and that do and will live upon it. No other people can have it, and we can have no other kingdom until we are prepared to inhabit this eternally. (*Journal of Discourses* 3:372)

Brigham Young further states:

It reads that the spirit goes to God who gave it. Let me render this scripture a little plainer; when the spirits leave their bodies they are in the presence of our Father and God, they are prepared then to see, hear and understand spiritual things. But where is the spirit world? It is incorporated within this celestial system. Can you see it with your natural eyes? No. Can you see spirits in this room? No. Suppose the Lord should touch your eyes that you might see, could you then see the spirits? Yes, as plainly as you now see bodies, as did the servant of Elijah. If the Lord would permit it, and it was his will that it should be done you could see the spirits that have departed from this world, as plainly as you now see bodies with your natural eyes. (*Discourses of Brigham Young*, pp. 376-77)

Other prophets have taught that, when permitted, those in the spirit world can see us, are often disappointed in our actions, and are sometimes sent to visit us with warnings, encouragement, and messages from God. The most important thing to remember is that only the physical body is dead. The eternal spirit continues to live. For the sake of discussion we will consider three states in the spirit world: paradise, spirit prison, and hell. Although all of the spirits are mingling together (as we are here on earth), there are places the spirits of the wicked cannot go, there are limitations on those who have not received the gospel, and there are varying grades of righteous spirits. (See *Discourses of Brigham Young* p. 377)

**Paradise** is a place of peace and rest from the temptations of Satan. President George Q. Cannon said:

We will also receive a great amount of reward as we go along, but not a fulness. Those who do not obey Satan in this life, when they die are freed from his power. They dwell in the paradise of God, and Satan has no power over them. Those who do obey Satan and are his servants in this life will, when they leave here, still be his servants, and he will have power over them. So it will be as we go along. (*Collected Discourses*, Vol.4, January 14, 1894)

Who will go to Paradise? Those who have passed the test of mortality and are awaiting the resurrection so they can enter the celestial kingdom. There are three groups: 1. Little children who die before they arrive at the age of accountability. Joseph Smith saw in vision that they were heirs of the celestial kingdom (see D&C 137:10). 2. Those who are mentally handicapped, although they live beyond the age of eight, since their minds do not develop to a point of accountability (see Alma 29:5; D&C 29:50). They will be heirs of the celestial kingdom. 3. Baptized members of the Church who endure faithfully to the end. President Joseph Fielding Smith wrote:

RIGHTEOUS GO TO PARADISE. It is the righteous who go to paradise. It is the righteous who cease from those things that trouble. Not so with the wicked. They remain in torment. They have their anguish of soul intensified, if you please, when they get on the other side, because they are constantly recalling to mind their evil deeds. They are aware of their neglected opportunities, privileges in which they might have served the Lord and received a reward of restfulness instead of a reward of punishment. And so they remain in torment until the time comes for their deliverance.[...]

The righteous, those who have kept the commandments of the Lord, are not shut up in any such place, but are in happiness in paradise. They cease from all this trouble, and trial, and tribulation, and anguish of soul. They are free from all these torments, because they have been true and faithful to their covenants.

DIVISIONS IN THE SPIRIT WORLD. All spirits of men after death return to the spirit world. There, as I understand it, the righteous — meaning those who have been baptized and who have been faithful — are gathered in one part and all the others in another part of the spirit world. This seems to be true from the vision given to President Joseph F. Smith and found in Gospel Doctrine. (*Doctrines of Salvation*, Vol.2, p.229 -30, all capitalization in the original)

What are the spirits of the righteous doing in Paradise? They are preaching to the spirits in Spirit Prison (see D&C 138:30-37), they continue perfecting themselves (since no one but Jesus was totally perfect when He died), and they learn at a greatly increased rate. Joseph Fielding Smith gave us something to seriously consider. He taught:

President Brigham Young declared that "every man and woman who has talent and hides it will be called a slothful servant. Improve day by day upon the capital you have. In proportion as we are capacitated to receive, so it is our duty to do." He also said, "I shall not cease learning while I live, nor when I arrive in the spirit world, but shall there learn with greater facility; and when I again receive my body, I shall learn a thousand times more in a thousand times less time; and then I do not mean to cease learning." Add to all this unlimited possibility the fact that our former knowledge, which was taken away, shall be returned, as taught by President Joseph F. Smith. (See Saturday Night Thoughts.) This being so, and there is no reasonable thought to oppose it, then we shall have a wonderful fund of information on which to build, for who knows how long we were learning in the eternity already past when we walked with God our Father? (*The Way to Perfection*, p.10)

There are many other church leaders who have taught

that, for the righteous in paradise, the veil that was placed over our minds (so we could learn to live by faith during our mortal testing period) will be removed and we will remember our pre-mortal life (see Parley P. Pratt: *Key to the Science of Theology* p. 129). There is much to be revealed as to how and when this shall happen. For our discussion, we need only know that those in Paradise are freed from Satan's evil influence, they continue their labors in preaching the gospel, and they continue perfecting themselves.

**Spirit Prison** — Who goes to the Spirit Prison? Those who have not had a chance, here on earth, to accept or reject the gospel. The probationary test of mortality has not been passed, so their opportunity to exercise their agency to accept or reject the gospel will continue. If a member of the church was not valiant during mortality, but had very limited or no opportunities to learn, he or she will continue to be taught in the Spirit Prison. Will Satan have power over the people in Spirit Prison? Brigham Young answered that question:

> If we are faithful to our religion, when we go into the spirit world, the fallen spirits — Lucifer and the third part of the heavenly hosts that came with him, and the spirits of wicked men who have dwelt upon this earth, the whole of them combined will have no influence over our spirits. Is not that an advantage? Yes. All the rest of the children of men are more or less subject to them, and they are subject to them as they were while here in the flesh. (*Discourses of Brigham Young*, p. 379)

What will the spirits in prison be doing? Learning the gospel and then waiting for endowed people on earth to perform the saving and exalting ordinances for them in the temples.

Will they still have a veil over their minds? Logic would

suggest that if the veil was placed there, blocking our memory of our pre-mortal past so we could learn to live by faith, and the test hasn't yet been successfully passed, then the veil would still be in place. The term "spirit prison" sometimes conjures up a vision of a person standing behind bars. The prison in the spirit prison is not one of bars but one of restrictions which limit the progress and movement of those who have not embraced the gospel. Ignorance imprisons us here as it does the spirits in prison. Bad habits and addictions take away our freedoms here as it does there. Violation of the laws of God damns (i.e. stops) us here as it does over there. In reality, the test of mortality continues for those in Spirit Prison the same as it does for those who are still alive in mortality.

**Hell** — For the sake of separating the good, honorable spirits of the dead who lived according to the best light and knowledge they had from those who sought evil all their lives, I choose to separate the Spirit Prison from another part of that prison which I call "Hotel Hell." "Hotel" because it is temporary between death and the resurrection. "Hell forever" or outer darkness or perdition will be the permanent residence of the sons of perdition and the devil.

Who will go to Hotel Hell? The scriptures are clear that unless we repent, we will have to suffer for our own sins (see D&C 19:16-17; 29:17; Alma 11:40-41 for examples). Some have the mistaken idea that only the murderers and the sons of perdition will suffer in hotel hell. While those vile characters will certainly be there, others will temporarily be consigned to that awful fate. Elder James E. Talmage gave the best explanation of hell I have ever seen:

> Hell is no place to which a vindictive judge sends prisoners to suffer and to be punished principally for his glory; but it is a place prepared for the teaching, the disciplining of those who failed to learn here upon the earth what they would have

learned. True, we read of everlasting punishment, unending suffering, eternal damnation. That is a direful expression; but in his mercy the Lord has made plain what those words mean. 'Eternal punishment' he says, is God's punishment, for he is eternal; and that condition or state or possibility will ever exist for the sinner who deserves and really needs such condemnation; but this does not mean that the individual sufferer or sinner is to be eternally and everlastingly made to endure and suffer. No man will be kept in hell longer than is necessary to bring him to a fitness for something better. When he reaches that stage, the prison doors will open and there will be rejoicing among the hosts who welcome him into a better state. The Lord has not abated in the least what he has said in earlier dispensations concerning the operation of this law and his gospel, but he has made clear unto us his goodness and mercy through it all, for it is his glory and his work to bring about the immortality and eternal life of man. (*Conference Report*, April 1930, p. 97)

Hotel Hell is a place where people will balance the scales of justice themselves because they would not repent and take advantage of the Savior's sacrifice. Even for those who suffer in hell, the Atonement of Christ seems to have some cleansing effect.

The dead who repent will be redeemed, through obedience to the ordinances of the house of God, And after they have paid the penalty of their transgressions, and **are washed clean**, shall receive a reward according to their works, for they are heirs of salvation. (D&C 138:58-59, emphasis added)

How much power does Satan have over the people in Hotel Hell? Total! Amulek taught: "For behold, if ye have procrastinated the day of your repentance even until death, behold, ye have become subjected to the spirit of the devil, and he doth seal you his; therefore, the Spirit of the Lord hath withdrawn from you, and hath no place in you, and the **devil hath all power over you**; and this is the final state of the wicked" (Alma 34:35, emphasis added).

After payment has been made for the sins of those in Hotel Hell (excepting those destined to become Sons of Perdition), the prison doors are opened and they will move into a place of learning and progression. Part of your responsibility as a missionary is to warn members of the Church to avoid doing those things which would require future payment in Hotel Hell. In describing your role as missionaries, the Lord said: "Behold, I send you out to reprove the world of all their unrighteous deeds, and to teach them of a judgment which is to come" (D&C 84:87). Our warning voice is not to be one of "hellfire and damnation" like so many others use. "And let your preaching be the warning voice, every man to his neighbor, in mildness and in meekness" (D&C 38:41).

We have only briefly touched on the glories which await us if we are faithful and the frightening prospects of the punishments, if we are not. Yours is the signal honor of being able to teach these and many other comforting doctrine to the peoples of the world. Learn so that you might give even what the Lord has revealed.

*Chapter 23*

# THE PLAN OF SALVATION – RESURRECTION AND JUDGMENT

We have lightly considered the pre-earth life, the purpose of earth life, death and the spirit world, and now we will conclude our study of the plan of salvation by briefly touching on the doctrine of resurrection and judgment. Before beginning the sequence of the different resurrections, answer the question: why should we be resurrected at all? If you will remember the chapter on "My Gospel" you may recall that we were born into mortality so we could die. We die so we can be resurrected. We will be resurrected so we can stand judgment for our thoughts, words, and actions. We will be judged to determine what kingdom of glory we are prepared to live in for the rest of eternity.

There are many places in scripture which touch on the resurrection. None is more complete than Doctrine and Covenants 88:96-102. We will discuss that passage verse by verse so you can get a clear mind-vision of what the Lord has revealed. The number before each paragraph will be the verse number in Doctrine and Covenants 88 unless otherwise stated:

96 "And the saints that are upon the earth, who are alive, shall be quickened and be caught up to meet him." If the Second Coming were to happen today, what would happen to you? If you were living a telestial law (eat, drink, and be merry — or lower) you would be destroyed by fire. "And every corruptible thing, both of man, or of the beasts of the field, or of the fowls of the heavens, or of the fish of the sea, that dwells upon all the face of the earth, shall be consumed" (D&C 101:24). If you were living a terrestrial law (good and honorable people) or higher, you would be "quickened" and caught up into the clouds of heaven. That quickening is also called "transfiguration." That is the temporary protecting of your body by the Holy Ghost to prevent you from being burned when you come into the presence of God. When Moses saw God, he was transfigured. He explained: "But now mine own eyes have beheld God; but not my natural, but my spiritual eyes, for my natural eyes could not have beheld; for I should have withered and died in his presence; but his glory was upon me; and I beheld his face, for I was **transfigured** before him" (Moses 1:11, emphasis added).

Transfiguration is not the same as translation or resurrection. Blood is running through your veins here on earth, blood will still be running through your veins when you are transfigured, and blood will continue to run through your veins when you return to the earth to begin the Millennium. How long will you continue to be mortal? Until you reach the age of a tree — which is one hundred years of age (see Isaiah 65:20). What will happen then? You'll be resurrected or changed "in the twinkling of an eye."

In that day an infant shall not die until he is old;
and his life shall be as the age of a tree;

And when he dies he shall not sleep, that is to say in the earth, but shall be changed in the twinkling of an eye, and shall be caught up, and his rest shall be glorious" (D&C 101:30-31). What if you have died before the Second Coming?

97 And they who have slept in their graves shall come forth, for their graves shall be opened; and they also shall be caught up to meet him in the midst of the pillar of heaven —

98 They are Christ's, the first fruits, they who shall descend with him first, and they who are on the earth and in their graves, who are first caught up to meet him; and all this by the voice of the sounding of the trump of the angel of God.

All of those people who have died since the resurrection of Christ, who lived a celestial law, will come forth to meet Him in the clouds of heaven. In fact, they will be resurrected before we, who are living, are transfigured and caught up (see 1 Thessalonians 4:16-17). This is called by modern prophets "the morning of the first resurrection" and means you will be resurrected with a body suited to dwell in celestial glory. No matter when you are resurrected, at the Second Coming or later, if you come forth with a celestial body, you will come forth in the morning of the first resurrection. We will discuss later how you recognize your celestial body.

Following the resurrection of those who are celestial and who died before the Second Coming will come the resurrection of those destined for the terrestrial kingdom.

99 And after this another angel shall sound, which is the second trump; and then cometh the redemption of those who are Christ's at his coming; who have received their part in that prison which is prepared for them, that they might receive the gospel, and be judged according to men in the flesh.

According to Section 76:71-80, these were good and honorable people that never really embraced the fulness of the gospel and hence were lacking in the saving and exalting ordinances. Even when taught in the spirit world, these people were still not valiant in their testimony of Christ. Their glory will surpass anything we can imagine, but will fall short of celestial glory.

The modern prophets have termed this resurrection as "the afternoon of the first resurrection." It will commence after the celestial beings have been resurrected and then continue throughout the millennium.

The next major division in the resurrection will be that of those destined to go to the telestial kingdom.

> 100 And again, another trump shall sound, which is the third trump; and then come the spirits of men who are to be judged, and are found under condemnation;
>
> 101 And these are the rest of the dead; and they live not again until the thousand years are ended, neither again, until the end of the earth.

Their mortal lives will unhappily end by being burned at the beginning of the millennium, if they have not already died. They will spend a thousand years and "a little season" until the "end of the earth" in "hotel hell." There, as we have discussed, they will be paying for their own sins and learning to control themselves, because they refused to do so while alive in mortality. These people gave themselves to carnality, sensuality, and lusts of the flesh while they lived, and therefore failed to develop a body which could withstand celestial glory.

The final group remaining to be resurrected will be those sorry people who followed Christ in the pre-earth "war in heaven" but, after embracing the fulness of the gospel here on earth, were overcome by the devil and openly defied and denied the power of God (read D&C 76:30-49). These are the dread "sons of Perdition" who will suffer eternally in Outer Darkness.

102 "And another trump shall sound, which is the fourth trump, saying: There are found among those who are to remain until that great and last day, even the end, who shall remain filthy still." They qualify for a resurrected body because of the Atonement of Christ, but merit no kingdom of glory because they were unwilling to enjoy one.

What determines which kingdom we inherit? The Lord clearly states earlier in Section 88:21-24:

> And they who are not sanctified through the law which I have given unto you, even the law of Christ, must inherit another kingdom, even that of a terrestrial kingdom, or that of a telestial kingdom.
>
> For he who is not able to abide the law of a celestial kingdom cannot abide a celestial glory.
>
> And he who cannot abide the law of a terrestrial kingdom cannot abide a terrestrial glory.
>
> And he who cannot abide the law of a telestial kingdom cannot abide a telestial glory; therefore he is not meet for a kingdom of glory. Therefore he must abide a kingdom which is not a kingdom of glory.

The standard is unmistakably clear. Whatever level of law a person chooses to obey will determine what kingdom he or she goes into. Elder Bruce R. McConkie gave an analogy which clarifies the process:

> In a real though figurative sense, the book of life is the record of the acts of men as such record is written in their own bodies. It is the record engraven on the very bones, sinews, and flesh of the mortal body. That is, every thought, word, and deed has an affect on the human body; all these leave their marks, marks which can be read by Him who is Eternal as easily as the words in a book can be read.

By obedience to telestial law men obtain telestial bodies; terrestrial law leads to terrestrial bodies; and conformity to celestial law — because this law includes the sanctifying power of the Holy Ghost — results in the creation of a body which is clean, pure, and spotless, a celestial body. (D. & C. 88:16-32.) When the book of life is opened in the day of judgment (Rev. 20:12-15), men's bodies will show what law they have lived. The Great Judge will then read the record of the book of their lives; the account of their obedience or disobedience will be written in their bodies. (*Mormon Doctrine*, p.97)

Carrying the analogy a little further, in a very figurative sense so we can understand, let's say celestial marks are triangles, terrestrial marks are circles, and telestial marks are squares. Every thought we think, word we say, or act we do leaves a mark that is a triangle, circle, or square on our bodies. Since none of us are completely celestial, the triangular marks on our body are mixed with circles and squares. How then will we be judged? Remember, in verse 21 the Lord referred to the "sanctifying power of law of Christ" — in other words, whenever we partake worthily of the sacrament, the blood of Christ acts as an invisible mark eraser. All marks that are not triangles are erased when we partake of the sacrament worthily following complete repentance.

But even then, we are not totally covered with triangular marks. What will happen in the resurrection? The Lord reveals:

They who are of a celestial spirit shall receive the same body which was a natural body; even ye shall receive your bodies, and your glory shall be that glory by which your bodies are quickened.

Ye who are **quickened by a portion** of the celestial glory shall then receive of the same, **even a fulness**.

And they who are quickened by a portion of the terrestrial glory shall then receive of the same, even a fulness.

And also they who are quickened by a portion of the telestial glory shall then receive of the same, even a fulness.

And they who remain shall also be quickened; nevertheless, they shall return again to their own place, to enjoy that which they are willing to receive, because they were not willing to enjoy that which they might have received. (D&C 88:28-32, emphasis added)

So if you are "quickened by a portion" (i.e. have partially, but not completely, developed a celestial body), you'll receive a fulness. Taking the analogy of marks one step further (for illustration purposes only!), we know that "likes attract" (see D&C 88:40). Therefore at the time of the resurrection of the celestials (remember this is only figurative!) a huge triangular magnet passes over the earth. All those with triangular marks are quickened and caught up. There is no magnetic pull between a triangular magnet and circular or square marks.

Following the resurrection of those with triangular marks, a huge circular magnet passes over the whole earth. Those who are of a terrestrial nature (have circular marks) will be quickened and caught up. Those with square marks would very much like to arise at this time, but there is no magnetic pull between a circular magnet and their square marks.

After spending a thousand years in "hotel hell," those with square marks will be quickened and caught up when the square magnet passes over the width and breath of the earth. Following that, even those who are sons of perdition (not Satan and the one-third part of those hosts of heaven who rebelled — they will never have the opportunity to have a physical body), will be quickened and caught up to be judged, and then sent to a place of no glory because they refused to enjoy a kingdom of glory.

When you get your resurrected body, it will be obvious if you have qualified for the Celestial Kingdom because your body will have the natural power to procreate. All other bodies assigned to different kingdoms will not have the procreation power in their resurrected bodies. Reread Doctrine and Covenants 88:28; 131:1-4; and 132:15-17 for further documentation. Read Doctrine and Covenants 132:19-25 for enlightenment concerning the powers in a resurrected, exalted body.

One last analogy to clarify the doctrine of kingdoms. Each kingdom (according to D&C 88:21-24) has a glory associated with it, other than outer darkness, which has no glory. Perhaps we might assign a temperature to each kingdom, according to Paul's analogy of the celestial kingdom being like unto the sun, the terrestrial to the moon, and the telestial to the stars (see 1 Corinthians 15:40-42). Let's say the telestial kingdom is heat rated at 5,000 degrees, the terrestrial at 10,000 degrees, and the celestial is 100,000 degrees. We are resurrected with a body suited for the glory of the kingdom into which we will spend eternity.

Could a person in the telestial kingdom ever (worlds without end) go to the terrestrial kingdom? No! Why? Because his or her body couldn't withstand the glory. Isn't that exactly what the Lord revealed speaking of those in the telestial kingdom? "And they shall be servants of the Most High; but where God and Christ dwell they cannot come, worlds without end" (D&C 76:112). President Spencer W. Kimball taught:

> **No progression between kingdoms.** After a person has been assigned to his place in the kingdom, either in the telestial, the terrestrial, or the

celestial, or to his exaltation, he will never advance from his assigned glory to another glory. That is eternal! That is why we must make our decisions early in life and why it is imperative that such decisions be right. (*The Teachings of Spencer W. Kimball*, p.50)

Can a person in a higher kingdom visit those in a lower kingdom? Yes! Because their bodies (suited for the higher temperatures) can easily withstand the glory of a lower kingdom. The Lord so taught:

These [telestial beings] are they who receive not of his fulness in the eternal world, but of the Holy Spirit through the ministration of the terrestrial;

And the terrestrial through the ministration of the celestial.

And also the telestial receive it of the administering of angels who are appointed to minister for them, or who are appointed to be ministering spirits for them; for they shall be heirs of salvation. (D&C 76:86-88)

If our analogy is correct, you can see the logic behind what the Lord revealed to Joseph Smith and the President Kimball. So it becomes an absolutely essential task for us to consciously put "triangular marks" on our body. Although repentance and the sacrament erase the circular and square marks, it does not automatically put triangular marks in their places. The absence of circular and square marks will not get a person into the celestial kingdom.

By daily striving to live the gospel, a person not only puts triangular marks on his or her body, but begins to develop their "fundamental part" (see below) into a triangular shape. Joseph Smith taught:

There is no fundamental principle belonging to a human system that ever goes into another in this world or the world to come; I care not what the theories of men are. We have the testimony that God will raise us up, and he has the power to do it. If anyone supposes that any part of our bodies, that is, the fundamental parts thereof, ever goes into another body, he is mistaken. (*History of the Church*, Vol. 5:339)

Perhaps this is what Elder Dallin H. Oaks had in mind when he taught:

> From such teachings we conclude that the Final Judgment is not just an evaluation of a sum total of good and evil acts — what we have *done.* It is an acknowledgment of the final effect of our acts and thoughts — what we have *become.* It is not enough for anyone just to go through the motions. The commandments, ordinances, and covenants of the gospel are not a list of deposits required to be made in some heavenly account. The gospel of Jesus Christ is a plan that shows us how to become what our Heavenly Father desires us to become. ("The Challenge to Become," *Ensign*, Nov. 2000, 32)

When we arrive at the final judgment, if we have become like God by living the laws which God gave us in the pre-earth life and in mortality, we have qualified for the celestial kingdom. Then the desire of our hearts voiced in the pre-earth life, to become like God, will have been realized. The message you will take to the world is to begin now to consciously evolve into the kind of a being that God is, so that we can live where God lives. That is the grand vision of the entirety of the great plan of happiness or the plan of salvation. Therefore, every waking moment of mortality should be a conscious effort to "Learn of me, and listen to my words; walk in the meekness of my Spirit, and you shall have peace in me" (D&C 19:23).

Can you see more clearly now what the Savior meant when He taught the Nephites: "Therefore, what manner of men ought ye to be? Verily I say unto you, even as I am" (3 Nephi 27:27)? It doesn't matter whether the people you enlighten are currently members of the Church or not. Every son or daughter of God will have to know and understand these principles if they are to achieve their divine potential. You are entrusted to teach them. Don't become discouraged or slack off. Eternal lives of our Father's children depend on your success.

*Chapter 24*

# RETURNING HOME
# WITH HONOR

From the beginning of your mission, it may seem like a very long time before you'll be returning home. But that isn't the case. As you lose yourself in the work, the end will come before you are ready. In order not to look back with regrets, you will need to resolve to do certain things from the very start of your mission.

Keep your mission in eternal perspective. According to God's method of marking time, one day with God is equal to one thousand years on earth (see Abraham 3:4). Therefore one year on earth is equivalent to one minute and twenty-six seconds in God's time! Your eighteen month mission (for sisters) is equal to two minutes and eight seconds! Your twenty-four month mission is equal to two minutes and fifty-two seconds for Elders! You don't have one second to waste.

Live just one day at a time. Don't try to live your whole mission all at once. Just be obedient one day at a time. Be diligent and faithful one day at a time. Take advantage of every opportunity to lift and build those you work with. Soon enough you'll be looking back at your mission as a distant memory. Too many missionaries anticipate the end of their missions only to discover that they have daydreamed away one of the truly memorable opportunities of a life time.

One young Elder who served with us had his wall almost covered with numbers starting at 138 and counting down to zero. When I questioned him about it, he said he was doing the "D&C countdown." Starting one hundred thirty-eight days before the end of his mission, he would read one section each day — starting at the end of the Doctrine and Covenants and working towards the front. That seemed fairly innocent, except he was always looking towards the end of his mission. Over four months later, when he completed his mission, I asked him if he thought that was a good idea. He tearfully said he wished he hadn't ever started such a project. He said with his eye continually focused on the end of his mission, he had missed some of the fun and wonderful experiences associated with those final months. Now he wanted to know if he could extend his mission so he could "do it up right" this time. Of course that wasn't possible, so he returned home somewhat disappointed that he hadn't followed the Savior's injunction to "Take therefore no thought for the morrow: for the morrow shall take thought for the things of itself. Sufficient unto the day is the evil thereof" (Matthew 6:34).

Another foolish young elder was sure that is was just a funny, innocent pastime to participate in the "Noah Days" game. On his wall was a descending string with numbers starting at forty and sequencing down to zero. At the top of the string was a make-shift ark. Each day, beginning at the fortieth day before his release, he would move the ark one notch down the string. Again I cautioned him against focusing on the end of his mission and missing some of the memory-creating experiences every faithful missionary has during those last weeks and months. He thought he knew better. It wasn't until his exit interview that he realized that his little game was neither fun or innocent. While others from his MTC group were recounting what they had experienced during the last couple of months, this young elder was quietly contemplating what he might have enjoyed but had missed because his focus was in the wrong place. Brigham Young said:

> I would say to my young friends and to the middle-aged brethren, though I believe all who are going may be called young men, that if you go on a mission to preach the gospel with lightness and frivolity in your hearts, looking for this and that, and to learn what is in the world, and not having your minds riveted — yes, I may say riveted — on the cross of Christ, you will go and return in vain. Go forth weeping, bearing precious seed, full of the power of God, and full of faith to heal the sick even by the touch of your hand, rebuking and casting out foul spirits, and causing the poor among men to rejoice, and you will return bringing your sheaves with you. If you do not go in this way your mission will not be very profitable to yourselves nor to the people. I wish you to bear this in mind. (*Journal of Discourses*, Vol.12, pp.33-34)

We found that, as difficult as it is, if the missionaries would live every day as though it were the last of the mission, they could look back without regret when the final day arrived. When you arise in the morning, tell yourself this is the last day you have to serve. Then go to as though it was your last day. Build, lift, and strengthen everyone you meet. Resolve to leave everyone better than you found them. Even if it is just a smile or a friendly word, consciously decide to do as Jesus did. Luke records: "How God anointed Jesus of Nazareth with the Holy Ghost and with power: **who went about doing good**, and healing all

that were oppressed of the devil; for God was with him"
(Acts 10:38, emphasis added). If we do what Jesus did, then
we will enjoy the same promise that He had (that God will
be with us).

It will be no easy task to stay focused on the work at
hand. It will require both you and your companion
constantly reminding each other. As you walk or ride
between appointments, as you break for lunch, as you relax
in your apartment at the end of the day, let your
conversation be about things concerning the gospel and
missionary work. Talk of girls (or guys), school, work, post-
mission plans, family, and the like, will only detract you
from your missionary focus. Keep those issues to a
minimum.

One technique used by our missionaries which seemed
to help was the challenge to prepare for a PPI (personal
priesthood interview) with the Savior at the end of their
service. The challenge I gave them was, when they went to
the temple the last week of their mission, to spend some
time in the Celestial Room. In quiet contemplation, they
were to review in their minds their entire missions. What
they had learned, who they had taught, experiences that
had enjoyed and those they just suffered through. They
were to figuratively put their arms around their mission
and then humbly ask the Savior if He accepted their efforts
as a mission well served.

When we first started the practice, some were very
concerned that, because of lack of diligence and obedience
during the early days of their missions, the Savior might not
accept their missions. One particular young elder
characterizes the experience of many. He reported during his
exit interview that he had not been faithful and diligent
during the early months of his mission. When I issued the
challenge he was sure his efforts would not be acceptable. He
said that he knew I would ask him to report his experience so

he sat in the celestial room for quite a while trying to figure out how to avoid reporting his experience. Finally he decided that he may as well find out whether he was rejected. As he started to mentally review his mission, he said he could only remember the rules he had broken, the road trips he had taken, the times he hadn't acted like a missionary.

Then some of the experiences he had enjoyed started coming to mind. Then he remembered a family he and his companion had baptized, and the list of good things began to grow. He stated that when he completed his review, he still thought the bad parts outweighed the good. Humbly he bowed his head and offered a silent prayer asking for forgiveness for the things he shouldn't have done and a confirmation of the Savior's acceptance. Then this large, athletic elder began to weep. He said, through the tears, "President, you didn't prepare me for what happened next. When I ended my prayer, I silently waited for the rejection manifestation. It didn't come. Instead it was like two huge arms of pure love reached out and embraced me. I felt like my bones would melt inside my body." He then concluded: "President, I don't know how or why He did it, but I have a sure knowledge that the Savior accepted my mission as well served!" The Spirit was testifying to me that what he was reporting actually happened and was true.

Now all the blessings promised to the faithful were his for the claiming if he continued faithful. You might recall the verbal interchange between the Savior and the rich young man who wanted to know what he had to do to get eternal life. Mark describes it best:

> And when he was gone forth into the way, there came one running, and kneeled to him, and asked him, Good Master, what shall I do that I may inherit eternal life?
>
> And Jesus said unto him, Why callest thou me good? there is none good but one, that is, God.

Thou knowest the commandments, Do not commit adultery, Do not kill, Do not steal, Do not bear false witness, Defraud not, Honour thy father and mother.

And he answered and said unto him, Master, all these have I observed from my youth.

Then Jesus beholding him loved him, and said unto him, One thing thou lackest: go thy way, sell whatsoever thou hast, and give to the poor, and thou shalt have treasure in heaven: and come, take up the cross, and follow me.

And he was sad at that saying, and went away grieved: for he had great possessions.

And Jesus looked round about, and saith unto his disciples, How hardly shall they that have riches enter into the kingdom of God!

And the disciples were astonished at his words. But Jesus answereth again, and saith unto them, Children, how hard is it for them that trust in riches to enter into the kingdom of God!

It is easier for a camel to go through the eye of a needle, than for a rich man to enter into the kingdom of God.

And they were astonished out of measure, saying among themselves, Who then can be saved?

And Jesus looking upon them saith, With men [it is] impossible, but not with God: for with God all things are possible.

Then Peter began to say unto him, Lo, we have left all, and have followed thee.

And Jesus answered and said, Verily I say unto you, There is no man that hath left house, or brethren, or sisters, or father, or mother, or wife, or children, or lands, for my sake, and the gospel's,

But he shall receive an hundredfold now in this time, houses, and brethren, and sisters, and mothers, and children, and lands, with persecutions; and in the world to come eternal life. (Mark 10:17-30)

It would be worth your time to seriously think about the Savior's promised rewards for a mission. Peter in essence asked, "We've left everything and gone on a mission. What's in it for us?" (see verse 28). The Savior, Whose name is also "the Truth," and who cannot lie, said every man who leaves the comforts of home, serves and honorable mission and endures faithfully to the end shall have (here in mortality): 1. One hundred fold in houses and lands (in other words physical wealth). That doesn't mean you'll be one hundred times richer than anyone else but it does mean that you will increase your earning capacity (without fear of losing your soul) by one hundred times over what you would have had if you had chosen not to go; 2. One hundred fold of wives and children (not that you'll have a hundred wives or a hundred children– which may not be a blessing) but that your relationship will be one hundred times better with your future spouse and children, if you will apply the principles you learned in the mission field, than if you hadn't gone; and 3. Eternal Life in the world to come. That is the highest degree of the celestial kingdom. Of course, if you fail to continue faithful, you put in jeopardy all of these promised blessings.

I have observed that how you finish your mission significantly impacts the way you will look back on your mission in the future. If you finish your mission on a high, then you'll remember the high points of your mission– the less desirable and negative parts of your mission will be blocked from your memory by the good and the uplifting things you experienced. However, if you finish on a low, then all the bad things that happened to you, all your disobedience, will come back to your memory and you'll know that you could have and should have done better. Wise missionaries will take this counsel and make sure you live your mission one day at a time so that you won't look back with regret.

Coming home, you have a distinct advantage. No one knows the changes you have made. Only you know how faithfully you have served. It is a time to recommit yourself to being as Christlike as you possibly can. It is a misnomer to label a **released** missionary as a **returned** missionary. The inference is that you can go back to what you were before your mission. That will never happen. When you left on your mission, the pre-mission ground on which you stood evaporated forever. One of the great tragedies of this generation is the number of released missionaries who try to return. They apparently abandon all the lessons they learned, all the gains they had made, all the spiritual rewards they had earned to try to find happiness in going back to look, act, talk, and be like they were before their missions. It would be like going to school for four years, enduring multiple exams, labs, papers, etc. in order to get an engineering degree, only to erase from your mind everything you learned as you enter the job market to secure employment. That would be foolish.

However, now the foundation for a successful life has been laid. The lessons you've learned, the principles which have successfully guided your life and helped you be a chosen missionary, the skills (like using the priesthood to bless, getting answers to prayers, learning to recognized and follow the prompting of the Spirit, etc.), and the maturity, both mental and spiritual, that you've won at such a price, are all keys to your future success.

*Chapter 25*

# YOUR LIFE-LONG
# MISSION

You may think it is premature to look forward to what life will be like after a mission. It is never too early to plan for success. If you are successful as a missionary, you'll discover that living the gospel is the mysterious key to "living after the manner of happiness" (2 Nephi 5:27). Regrettably, even many members of the church who have served missions are making the spiritually fatal mistake that the apostate Nephites made. Samuel the Lamanite explained to them,

> But behold, your days of probation are past; ye have procrastinated the day of your salvation until it is everlastingly too late, and your destruction is made sure; yea, for ye have sought all the days of your lives for that which ye could not obtain; and ye have **sought for happiness in doing iniquity**, which thing is contrary to the nature of that righteousness which is in our great and Eternal Head. (Helaman 13:38, emphasis added)

As you return home to continue life, you have the equivalent of fifty years of Church experience. The General

Authorities who presided over me, when I served as a mission president, said they had calculated that a well served mission was equal to fifty years of normal church service. Therefore you are, church-experience wise, about where your grandparents are if they didn't serve missions.

With that kind of a head start, there is no limit to what you can accomplish. If you have been observant, you will have discovered that holding a position in the mission field was not the criteria for success. Whether you are called to be a bishop, Relief Society president, or are just a "normal" member of the Church, you can have a tremendous impact on the rising generation. The Lord does not have an overabundance of people who can say, "Come follow me as I follow the Savior." Someone once asked the group I was in a thought-provoking question: "If you were the only Standard Works that people could read, and they imitated your every thought, word, and action, how Christlike would they be?" The more I focused on how well I was doing, the more convinced I became that I had a lot of improving to do.

As you return home at the completion of your mission, you can not only keep the cutting edge you've developed in the mission field, but improve upon it. How? It is simple! The gains you made in the mission field came as you daily read the scriptures, prayed multiple times each day, and served others. That same formula will keep you spiritually healthy when you return home. Add regular temple attendance, faithful payment of tithes and offerings, and service in the church, and you'll not have to worry about falling into forbidden paths.

Getting down on yourself for not being perfect is non-productive. Excusing yourself for less than Christlike behavior is growth-retarding. The very lessons you learned in the mission field, if consistently applied, will make you ultimately successful in marriage and in life. Let's list some of those lessons:

- In the mission field you will learn to treat everyone with respect, even when they differ from your beliefs. You will control your urge to argue or fight with them. Carried into marriage and family living, spouse or child abuse would virtually disappear from your future home.

- You will learn to clearly and understandably explain what you believe and to answer any questions which need clarifying. In your future home with your spouse and children, you would refrain from the ego-destroying, but frequently used, tactic of calling someone "stupid" for not understanding your directive or point of view. You would exercise Godly patience in helping others, who may not have the mental capacity you have, to grasp difficult concepts quickly without expressing frustration or lack of patience.

- You will learn how to read the scriptures and apply their teachings to your everyday life. If you continue that practice of daily scripture study, pondering its application, and dutifully applying its principles, your life will be as celestially manageable as possible in a corrupt world.

- In the mission field you will come to love and revere the Lord's living prophets and anxiously await their counsel and direction. If you continue to look to the mouthpieces of God, you will be among the relatively few who escape the holocaust leading up to the Second Coming of the Savior.

- You will endure more in serving your full time mission that you thought possible. The Lord will not push you beyond what He knows you are capable of handling — but it will be more than you think you are capable of handling. If you carry that same "finisher" attitude into your marriage and family life, divorce will not be an option for solving the problems you will face. What a blessing to know that you can endure whatever trials the Lord allows to come your way, and not only endure but grow and prosper by meeting and overcoming those challenges.

- You will learn while serving your mission that some problems can only be solved through prayer and fasting. As you are faced with the problems of life in marriage, family rearing, and professional life, you'll frequently use prayer to gain the insight necessary to be successful.

- As a missionary you'll learn the value of the priesthood in giving and getting blessings of comfort and direction. As a married person, the priesthood will become an indispensable tool in combating the evil influences which will constantly surround you and your family.

- During your mission you will have the opportunity to look into the private lives of many people — both members and investigators. You'll observe some things that really work well in marriage and family living, and many other things that always result in arguments and divisions. If you are wise, when you return home and begin your family life, you will religiously implement those Godly characteristics you noted in successful families and do all in your power to avoid those relationship-destroying characteristics you observed in other families. If you fail to "connect the dots," you will be destined to learn by sad experience with your own spouse and children. Jacob pleaded with his people to "learn with joy and not with sorrow" (Jacob 4:3) from the mistakes made by those who went before.

- Of necessity, during your mission you will learn to economize. The missionary allotment, although adequate to meet your needs, certainly will not make you rich. You will learn to live on much less than you thought possible. In a world drowning in debt, you will rise to the surface as one of the few wise enough to avoid stress-producing debt. You will learn as newly-marrieds to live on much less than you thought possible. What you may have seen as "needs" while growing up really fall into the "wants" category. Blessed is the young couple willing to live within their means, saving a little each month until they can afford the luxuries that many of their counterparts insisted on having from the beginning of their marriages, only to discover that the unbearable crush of unpayable debts may have destroyed their marriages.

- If you haven't seen it before, you will come face to face with the unmistakable reality that what Hollywood promotes as normal, isn't. If you are observant, you will see the relationship-destroying effects of infidelity or even flirting outside the marriage. You will see the devastation that follows divorce and the unhappiness to both former spouses and to all the children when the ways of the world (divorce and marry again at will) are adopted. It won't take much for you to determine that you are not going to prematurely enter into marriage and discover too late that you should have identified and resolved serious differences before making eternal commitments.

- With sorrow and heartache, you will observe first hand the tragedy of addiction of any kind. Food, drugs, alcohol, sex, entertainment, Internet, sleep, music, clothes, and a thousand other things can captivate, control, and suffocate their victims. You will sadly observe that those so addicted are the least free people on earth. When you return home, you will have your guard up against such addictions. With vigilance, you'll recognize Satan's evil addictive efforts before they become ingrained, and take necessary steps to avoid being caught with his "flaxen chords" which drag his victims down to a life of misery and endless woe (see 2 Nephi 26:22).

- Immersing yourself 24/7 in things that are eternally significant in the mission field will develop in your heart an unquenchable desire to live for eternity and not to be detoured by things that will fade into oblivion at death. You will see people who have devoted their entire lives in pursuit of riches, power, popularity, or other vain things Lehi saw in his vision of the tree of life (see 1 Nephi 8). When you return and commence your married life and career, there will be forces beckoning you to focus your undivided attention on the very things you observed first hand in the mission field. Hopefully you will be wise enough to see through the deceptive smoke-screen of the adversary and keep your attention focused on what the Lord has revealed as necessary to gain eternal life.

- Because it is difficult to live together with a companion and others without some friction, you will learn how to say "I'm sorry" — and really mean it — many times in the mission field. You will discover that being right isn't always as important as being unified so you can enjoy the presence of the Spirit. You will learn that most of the differences you have with companions aren't "right and wrong" issues but differences in personal preference. You will come to know the absolute truth of the Lord's challenge and warning: "I say unto you, be one; and if ye are not one ye are not mine" (D&C 38:27).

- Carrying into marriage that principle of compromise, you will discover that the three most conciliatory words in the English language are: "You're probably right!" Those three words will open the way for discussing your differences and finding a Christlike solution to your problems. Learning how to identify and solve problems before they grow into destructive differences will enable you to focus your attention on external problems rather than worrying endlessly about holding your marriage and family together.

- In the mission field you will soon discover that everyone isn't what he or she appears to be. Some people have split personalities spiritually. They appear to be one thing in church and in public and are entirely different in their private lives at home. Some of the most kind and mild-mannered people at church are the most abusive and tyrannical at home. If you are observant, you'll see how hypocritical that is and how devastatingly destructive it is to a spouse and children who can't reconcile the "Dr. Jekyll and Mr. Hyde" nature of their spouse or parent. You will gain an unquenchable desire to be "one" with yourself. What a pleasant experience to meet a person who can truthfully say: "What you see is what you get." He or she is the same no matter whether in the limelight at church or public or in the private confines of their own home. Strive to be like that.

- In the mission field you will learn to quickly assess any situation and then, without being commanded or asked, do whatever must be done to make the occasion successful. If you do the same thing in your home ward, your career, and your family, you will be one of the rare individuals whom the Lord can trust with great responsibility. The Lord declared:

    Verily I say, men should be anxiously engaged in a good cause, and do many things of their own free will, and bring to pass much righteousness;

For the power is in them, wherein they are agents unto themselves. And inasmuch as men do good they shall in nowise lose their reward.

But he that doeth not anything until he is commanded, and receiveth a commandment with doubtful heart, and keepeth it with slothfulness, the same is damned. (D&C 58:27-29)

- In the mission field you will have many opportunities to forgive others — even when they do not repent or ask for your forgiveness. Many rude people will give you directives where to go, they will wave at you with a limited number of fingers on one hand, they will refer to your parentage, and offer many other rude remarks designed to anger you. You will learn to ignore their inappropriate actions and forgive them as the Savior did. If you can take that same forgiving attitude into marriage, you can eliminate most of the argument-producing offenses which frequently occur as young married couples learn to adjust to each other.

- As a leader in the mission field, you will have the opportunity to learn to lead without abusing your power and without becoming prideful. The Lord revealed: "We have learned by sad experience that it is the nature and disposition of almost all men, as soon as they get a little authority, as they suppose, they will immediately begin to exercise unrighteous dominion" (D&C 121:39). Will you be one of the few who can be entrusted with power without letting it go to your head? Paul tried to correct the principles of pride in the local leadership of the Roman saints when he wrote, "For I say, through the grace given unto me, to every man that is among you, not to think of himself more highly than he ought to think; but to think soberly, according as God hath dealt to every man the measure of faith" (Romans 12:3).

If you can continue that servant-leadership attitude in marriage, the Lord promises that "thy scepter [will be] an unchanging scepter of righteousness and truth; and thy dominion shall be an everlasting dominion, and without compulsory means it shall flow unto thee forever and ever" (D&C 121:46), meaning that people will want you to govern them as the Savior governs us. Can you conceive of the peace and harmony that could and will exist in your home if you can learn to use the power of leadership the way the Savior does?

- You will discover in the mission field that there is considerably more that you don't know than what you do know. You will develop an attitude of willingness to be taught by anyone and everyone that God places in your path. You will develop a thirst for learning that continues to grow the more you learn.

If you maintain that sponge-like learning attitude you cannot begin to comprehend the visions and revelations you will receive. The Lord revealed:

For thus saith the Lord — I, the Lord, am merciful and gracious unto those who fear me, and delight to honor those who serve me in righteousness and in truth unto the end.

Great shall be their reward and eternal shall be their glory.

And to them will I reveal all mysteries, yea, all the hidden mysteries of my kingdom from days of old, and for ages to come, will I make known unto them the good pleasure of my will concerning all things pertaining to my kingdom.

Yea, even the wonders of eternity shall they know, and things to come will I show them, even the things of many generations.

And their wisdom shall be great, and their understanding reach to heaven; and before them the wisdom of the wise shall perish, and the understanding of the prudent shall come to naught.

For by my Spirit will I enlighten them, and by my power will I make known unto them the secrets of my will — yea, even those things which eye has not seen, nor ear heard, nor yet entered into the heart of man. (D&C 76:5-10)

Too often, in my Doctrine and Covenants classes at BYU, I see returned missionaries sitting in the back of the classroom with their arms folded sending the non-verbal message "teach me if you think you can!" Thankfully, most of them discover before too many class sessions that there is a wonderful gospel they haven't yet discovered. I hope I never get so omniscient that I can't learn from babes and people of lesser education and station than the one I am (or think I am) in.

With a little more thought, the lessons learned from the mission field can be multiplied as though they have no end, for indeed they do have no end. Your mission can be the greatest springboard for the rest of your life that the Lord could provide. Please don't view your mission as an eighteen month or two year period blanked out of your life. See it as what it is, the most intense pre-marriage and adult-life training session that God has provided for His faithful children.

*Chapter 26*

# RETURNING TO YOUR ETERNAL HOME WITH HONOR

Now we have come almost full circle. From the dawn of our pre-earth life, we have longed and worked for the privilege and honor of returning to the presence of our Heavenly Parents and enjoying with them Eternal Life. For this purpose you were born in the pre-earth life. For this purpose you were born into mortality. And for this same purpose we will be born (or raised) into a resurrected state.

As we ponder the trust that Heavenly Father has placed in us to be the chosen few who will help prepare the world for the Second Coming of Christ, we can understand why our lives seem to meet almost constant opposition. When the Savior comes, Satan and his followers will be cast into "Hotel Hell" for a thousand years. At the end of the Millennium will be a little season where Satan will be loosed in preparation for the "battle of the great God" (see D&C 88:111-115). You will be there but not as a mortal being. Long before that time you will have received your resurrected body but will be honored to participate in the final battle with evil.

During that battle, if there are casualties, they will be the mortals who will be alive on the earth at that time, as we are preceding the Second Coming. The ultimate casualties will be Satan and one-third part of the hosts of heaven who were cast out into the earth (see Revelation 12:4-9) following their abortive attempt to dethrone God in the pre-earth life. There will be a number of people who will have fallen from celestial blessings to the depths of outer darkness after having received their physical bodies and the fulness of the gospel. These are the mortal sons of perdition spoken of in scriptures (see D&C 76:30-49) and of whom it is stated that it would have been better for them if they had never been born.

Now, here we are standing as it were on the very edge of the most exciting time in all eternity. The numberless spirit children of our Heavenly Parents who have lived out their mortality on earth will present themselves for judgment. In the judgment it will not be the absence of evil that will qualify an individual for a seat in the celestial kingdom. At that moment everyone other than the sons of perdition will be clean. Now will come the time when the impact of everything we have experienced, from our pre-mortal birth, through the countless ages in pre-mortal schooling, through the relatively short mortal probationary period, through the post-mortal spirit world, will be noted. If we have truly internalized the characteristics which makes God what He is, then we will gain an exaltation with Him in the celestial kingdom.

If we have merely gone through the motions but have not seen the eternal value of living the kind of life that God lives, then we must be satisfied with a lesser kingdom, even that of a terrestrial order or a telestial order. By that time, the choice will have been made by each individual son or daughter of God, having had a full opportunity to accept or reject the fulness of the gospel of Jesus Christ. Not one person will be missed. Every good act will be rewarded.

Every wrong will have been paid for by the Atonement of Christ or by the suffering of the sinner.

The history of the earth will be reviewed by all, including the secret acts, thoughts, and the marvelous works of God. This will be done in order, considering, weighing, and judging each individual for each successive thousand year period. The Lord explained:

> And then shall the first angel again sound his trump in the ears of all living, and reveal the secret acts of men, and the mighty works of God in the first thousand years.
>
> And then shall the second angel sound his trump, and reveal the secret acts of men, and the thoughts and intents of their hearts, and the mighty works of God in the second thousand years —
>
> And so on, until the seventh angel shall sound his trump; and he shall stand forth upon the land and upon the sea, and swear in the name of him who sitteth upon the throne, that there shall be time no longer; and Satan shall be bound, that old serpent, who is called the devil, and shall not be loosed for the space of a thousand years. (D&C 88:108-110)

We have some glorious and some frightening times ahead before the Second Coming. Elder Neal A. Maxwell, in pondering future events, said:

> Yes, there will be wrenching polarization on this planet, but also the remarkable reunion with our colleagues in Christ from the city of Enoch. Yes, nation after nation will become a house divided, but more and more unifying Houses of the Lord will grace this planet. Yes, Armageddon lies ahead — but so does Adam-ondi-Ahman! (*Even As I Am*, p.121)

We are seeing the fulfillment of Elder Maxwell's prophetic insight. Nations are aligning themselves for or against the principles of freedom and righteousness. People seem to be polarizing. Up to this time there have been three groups: the Saints, the Aints, and the Complaints! Now the Lord seems to be saying to the complaints, "Make up your minds. Choose whether you will live like and with the saints or quit trying to hide behind the protective covering of the Church and show your true colors as one of the Aints." He foretold this many years ago:

> Behold, vengeance cometh speedily upon the inhabitants of the earth, a day of wrath, a day of burning, a day of desolation, of weeping, of mourning, and of lamentation; and as a whirlwind it shall come upon all the face of the earth, saith the Lord.
>
> And upon my house shall it begin, and from my house shall it go forth, saith the Lord;
>
> First among those among you, saith the Lord, who have professed to know my name and have not known me, and have blasphemed against me in the midst of my house, saith the Lord. (D&C 112:24-27)

Before the end arrives, those living in a Zion-like way will be the only ones not warring one with another.

> And it shall be called the New Jerusalem, a land of peace, a city of refuge, a place of safety for the saints of the Most High God;
>
> And the glory of the Lord shall be there, and the terror of the Lord also shall be there, insomuch that the wicked will not come unto it, and it shall be called Zion.
>
> And it shall come to pass among the wicked, that every man that will not take his sword against his neighbor must needs flee unto Zion for safety.
>
> And there shall be gathered unto it out of every nation under heaven; and it shall be the only people that shall not be at war one with another.

And it shall be said among the wicked: Let us not go up to battle against Zion, for the inhabitants of Zion are terrible; wherefore we cannot stand.

And it shall come to pass that the righteous shall be gathered out from among all nations, and shall come to Zion, singing with songs of everlasting joy. (D&C 45:66-71)

What must we do to qualify for the promised Divine protection? The Lord said:

Therefore, verily, thus saith the Lord, let Zion rejoice, for this is Zion — THE PURE IN HEART; therefore, let Zion rejoice, while all the wicked shall mourn.

For behold, and lo, vengeance cometh speedily upon the ungodly as the whirlwind; and **who shall escape it?**

The Lord's scourge shall pass over by night and by day, and the report thereof shall vex all people; yea, it shall not be stayed until the Lord come;

For the indignation of the Lord is kindled against their abominations and all their wicked works.

Nevertheless, **Zion shall escape if** she observe to do all things whatsoever I have commanded her.

But if she observe not to do whatsoever I have commanded her, I will visit her according to all her works, with sore affliction, with pestilence, with plague, with sword, with vengeance, with devouring fire.

Nevertheless, let it be read this once to her ears, that I, the Lord, have accepted of her offering; and if she sin no more none of these things shall come upon her;

And I will bless her with blessings, and multiply a multiplicity of blessings upon her, and upon her generations forever and ever, saith the

Lord your God. Amen. (D&C 97:21-28, emphasis added)

Now the stage is set. The members of the Church can, if they will, avoid the problems of the latter-day — in fact "Zion will rejoice while ALL the wicked shall mourn." If we don't escape it will be because we haven't been willing to follow the Lord's commandments and His leaders. We have a clear choice: repent and rejoice, or try to live in Babylon (which is spiritual wickedness — see D&C 133:14) and mourn with the wicked.

The Savior will appear many times to men and women here on the earth before making His grand appearance in the clouds of heaven — which we normally label "the Second Coming." He will appear to His saints in the temples (see Malachi 3:1; D&C 36:8; 133:2). He will make a grand appearance before one hundred million people at a great meeting at Adam-ondi-Ahman (see Daniel 7:9-14). Stewardships will be reported, instructions given, and preparations for the Second Coming will be put into full gear.

Yet another appearance will be to a beleaguered Jewish population who will have been holed-up in Jerusalem for forty-two months (three and a half years). The Jews will be protected by two prophets raised up to the Jewish nation, but finally destroyed by a portion of a world-wide army numbering 200,000,000 (see Revelation 9:16). After three and a half days of reveling over the dead bodies of these two prophets, the Lord will resurrect them (see Revelation 11:2-12). At that point, Christ and 144,000 high priests will appear on the Mount of Olives and save the Jewish nation (see Revelation 14:5; Zechariah 14; and D&C 45:51-53, and D&C 133:18). There will be many other appearances in addition to the three outlined (see D&C 133:20-21).

The appearance we generally refer to as the Second Coming, where the newly resurrected saints and those saints who have been transfigured will meet him in the clouds of heaven, is described in many places, but one will suit our purpose:

And it shall be said: Who is this that cometh down from God in heaven with dyed garments; yea, from the regions which are not known, clothed in his glorious apparel, traveling in the greatness of his strength?

And he shall say: I am he who spake in righteousness, mighty to save.

And the Lord shall be red in his apparel, and his garments like him that treadeth in the wine-vat.

And so great shall be the glory of his presence that the sun shall hide his face in shame, and the moon shall withhold its light, and the stars shall be hurled from their places.

And his voice shall be heard: I have trodden the wine-press alone, and have brought judgment upon all people; and none were with me;

And I have trampled them in my fury, and I did tread upon them in mine anger, and their blood have I sprinkled upon my garments, and stained all my raiment; for this was the day of vengeance which was in my heart.

And now the year of my redeemed is come; and they shall mention the loving kindness of their Lord, and all that he has bestowed upon them according to his goodness, and according to his loving kindness, forever and ever.

In all their afflictions he was afflicted. And the angel of his presence saved them; and in his love, and in his pity, he redeemed them, and bore them, and carried them all the days of old. (D&C 133:46-53)

As we rejoice in one of the greatest family reunions mentioned in all scripture, the Savior will direct our attention towards the earth.

> And prepare for the revelation which is to come, when the veil of the covering of my temple, in my tabernacle, which hideth the earth, shall be taken off, and all flesh shall see me together.
>
> And every corruptible thing, both of man, or of the beasts of the field, or of the fowls of the heavens, or of the fish of the sea, that dwells upon all the face of the earth, shall be consumed;
>
> And also that of element shall melt with fervent heat; and all things shall become new, that my knowledge and glory may dwell upon all the earth. (D&C 101:23-25)

Sometime before the actual Second Coming an earthquake will cause the continents to slide back into the position they occupied before they were divided in the days of Peleg, the great-grandson of Noah. The Lord shall utter forth His voice,

> And it shall be a voice as the voice of many waters, and as the voice of a great thunder, which shall break down the mountains, and the valleys shall not be found.
>
> He shall command the great deep, and it shall be driven back into the north countries, and the islands shall become one land;
>
> And the land of Jerusalem and the land of Zion shall be turned back into their own place, and the earth shall be like as it was in the days before it was divided. (D&C 133:22-24)

There are so many signs and wonders that you will see before the end of the world (which is scripturally defined as wickedness — see JST Matthew 1:4) comes. Joseph Fielding Smith taught:

RESTORATION OF THE EARTH. Joseph Smith gave this inspired summary of latter-day events: 'There shall be famine, and pestilence, and earthquake in divers places; and the prophets have declared that the valleys should rise; that the mountains should be laid low; that a great earthquake should be, in which the sun should become black as sack-cloth of hair, and the moon turn into blood; yea, the Eternal God hath declared that the great deep shall roll back into the north countries and that the land of Zion and the land of Jerusalem shall be joined together, as they were before they were divided in the days of Peleg. No wonder the mind starts at the sound of the last days!' (*Doctrines of Salvation*, Vol. 1, p. 84 - p. 85, all capital letter are in the original)

Hopefully this short recital of a few of the signs will motivate you to study more carefully what the Lord has revealed concerning His Coming. Don't be in too big a hurry. Study slowly and carefully and you'll start to get a feel for the sequence of future events.

The Savior's return ushers in the Millennium. For a thousand years, for the children born to mortals like yourself, "the earth shall be given unto them for an inheritance; and they shall multiply and wax strong, and their children shall grow up without sin unto salvation" (D&C 45:58). And when the children reach the age of a tree (100 years of age — see Isaiah 65:20), "when he dies he shall not sleep, that is to say in the earth, but shall be changed in the twinkling of an eye, and shall be caught up, and his rest shall be glorious" (D&C 101:31).

Then all of the difficult questions which those opposed to the church glory in throwing at you, as if your not being able to answer the questions would prove the church is not true, shall be answered. The Lord said:

Yea, verily I say unto you, in that day when the Lord shall come, he shall reveal all things —

Things which have passed, and hidden things which no man knew, things of the earth, by which it was made, and the purpose and the end thereof —

Things most precious, things that are above, and things that are beneath, things that are in the earth, and upon the earth, and in heaven. (D&C 101:32-34)

When we have the opportunity to have the Savior explain the purpose behind all of the trials and tribulations we have endured, then (if not before) we will be constrained to admit that God knew best. We will see that everything we thought was totally worthless was indeed necessary for our salvation and exaltation.

So prepare yourself for the wild ride ahead as we count down the days before the Second Coming. Fired with celestial vision, prophets for millennia have desired to live during our day. However, for reasons known to God alone, you have been privileged to occupy an honored position in His final kingdom. Watch and be careful. The adversary will not rest until he has destroyed all who will not heed the voice of the Lord and His servants. Those who will rise to the challenge will be honored at His Second Coming. "And I now give unto you a commandment to beware concerning yourselves, to give diligent heed to the words of eternal life" (D&C 84:43). You'll make it if you'll join the Lord's first team and not try to play both sides of the net.

*Chapter 27*

# ONE CHANCE TO SERVE – SERVE WITH HONOR

Over the years, in his customary attempt to distort the truth, Satan has whispered to the youth of the church that serving a mission is a right which automatically comes when a young man reaches age nineteen or a young woman twenty-one. Repeatedly the First Presidency has expressed the truth in saying that a mission is a privilege, not a right. They have outlined in some detail the moral worthiness, mental stability, and level of preparedness required by candidates applying for full time missionary service. If you are not familiar with the latest requirements, contact your bishop or stake president.

Even before the church was restored, the Lord outlined (several times) what was necessary to qualify for service in His soon-to-be organized kingdom. He said: "And faith, hope, charity and love, with an eye single to the glory of God, **qualify** him for the work" (D&C 4:5, emphasis added). It would be to your eternal benefit to study what the scriptures say about each of these five characteristic and see if you can strengthen them in your life, especially before entering into full time missionary service.

The fifth named attribute may cause you a little trouble, because it is a phrase rather than a single word. Analyzing the key words, however, gives you a starting place. What is "the glory of God?" The Lord defined His work and His glory to Moses thousands of years ago. "For behold, this is my work and my glory — to bring to pass the immortality and eternal life of man" (Moses 1:39). It is easy to verbalize: anything that moves a man or woman closer to qualifying for eternal life assists in promoting the glory of God. If your eye is single, then virtually everything you do leaves people better than you found them. Some missionaries mistakenly believe that they are not doing missionary work unless they are teaching discussions or preparing people for baptism. The Lord takes a much broader view. Virtually anything that influences a person to be more Christlike, whether member or not, whether interested in being taught or not, whether you'll ever meet them again or not, is missionary work. You don't know but what the smile, the word of encouragement, the roadside assistance will result, many years from now, in that person accepting the discussions from missionaries.

Although the five characteristics listed in verse five qualify you to serve, the additional character traits mentioned in verse six put you in a position to be most effective — not only in helping others progress but in maximizing the personal benefit of the mission. The Lord continued: "Remember faith, virtue, knowledge, temperance, patience, brotherly kindness, godliness, charity, humility, diligence" (D&C 4:6). So important are they that two of the characteristics are mentioned a second time: faith and charity. These characteristics are also mentioned by Peter as steps to making your calling and election sure (see 2 Peter 1:5-10).

You will likely know the Lord's definition of faith as written in Alma 32:21: "And now as I said concerning faith

— faith is not to have a perfect knowledge of things; therefore if ye have faith ye hope for things which are not seen, which are true." Faith is one of the deepest, most profound doctrines of the gospel. Take the hours necessary to study related passages from the Topical Guide and see what the Lord says about developing and strengthening your faith. You will not only benefit personally, but you will be better equipped to help those you teach develop this godly attribute.

Charity is also a profoundly deep attribute. Moroni was so impressed with his father's teaching concerning "faith, hope, and charity" (see Moroni 7), that he copied it into his own writings when his only possible audience would not be born for hundreds of years. He said:

And again, behold I say unto you that he cannot have faith and hope, save he shall be meek, and lowly of heart.

If so, his faith and hope is vain, for none is acceptable before God, save the meek and lowly in heart; and if a man be meek and lowly in heart, and confesses by the power of the Holy Ghost that Jesus is the Christ, he must needs have charity; for if he have not charity he is nothing; wherefore he must needs have charity.

And charity suffereth long, and is kind, and envieth not, and is not puffed up, seeketh not her own, is not easily provoked, thinketh no evil, and rejoiceth not in iniquity but rejoiceth in the truth, beareth all things, believeth all things, hopeth all things, endureth all things.

Wherefore, my beloved brethren, if ye have not charity, ye are nothing, for charity never faileth. Wherefore, cleave unto charity, which is the greatest of all, for all things must fail —

But **charity is the pure love of Christ**, and it

endureth forever; and whoso is found possessed of it at the last day, it shall be well with him.

Wherefore, my beloved brethren, pray unto the Father with all the energy of heart, that ye may be filled with this love, which he hath bestowed upon all who are true followers of his Son, Jesus Christ; that ye may become the sons of God; that when he shall appear we shall be like him, for we shall see him as he is; that we may have this hope; that we may be purified even as he is pure. Amen. (Moroni 7:43-48, emphasis added)

Although that is the most comprehensive and beautiful definition of charity and how to obtain it, there are several other definitions which shed additional light. One with which you may not be as familiar is: "And above all things, clothe yourselves with the bond of **charity**, as with a mantle, **which is the bond of perfectness and peace**" (D&C 88:125, emphasis added). You can tell when you are speaking or acting charitably if it increases the perfectness and enhances the peace of the people you are teaching or associating with. What a power you could be if you could start now, and for the rest of your life do only those things which promoted peace and perfection.

Can you see that just being away from home for two years doesn't even begin to qualify as serving an honorable mission? It will require all of the knowledge, power, and maturity you can muster. Even then you will fall miserably short. However, with the help of the Savior, you can and will succeed. Remember: "Without me, ye can do nothing!" (John 15:5).

Probably one of the most famous verses in the entire canon of scripture for Latter-day Saints is found in Doctrine and Covenants 18:10. "Remember the worth of souls is great in the sight of God." How great is the worth of a soul? Perhaps a little question and answer session will help you realize the magnitude of the work you are called to do.

Suppose, by some dark turn of events, that God had been taken captive by evil powers. They were going to execute Him unless a ransom was paid. If you had unlimited access to limitless wealth, how much ransom would you pay to free God? I suspect, if you seriously think about it, your answer would be, "I'd pay whatever was necessary to save God's life!" Now answer the question: "What is the potential of every person on earth?" Is it not to become like God in the eternal worlds?

God thought the individual and collective souls of His spirit children were of sufficient worth that He willingly sacrificed His Only Begotten Son to ransom us from death and hell (reread D&C 18:11-14; 2 Nephi 9:6-13).

Because of the worth of souls, God calls His sons and daughters on missions to preach the gospel (the saving vehicle) to His spirit children who were born without the fulness of truth. He said, "Wherefore, you are called to cry repentance unto this people" (D&C 18:14). Without repentance people cannot return to the presence of God, because "no unclean thing can dwell in the presence of God" (see 1 Nephi 10:21; Moses 6:57). Without the message you will take to the world, the people of the world can never be saved in the kingdom of God. That may sound a bit arrogant, and indeed it would be, except it is the Lord Himself who is making the pronouncement. He doesn't lie, but always tells it the way it is.

If you are called to a very challenging mission (and I don't know of a mission that doesn't have its challenges!) you may not have the opportunity of baptizing many people. At times you may be tempted to ask yourself if you are wasting your time and money. The Lord put that question into eternal perspective when He said: "And if it so be that you should labor all your days in crying repentance unto this people, and bring, save it be one soul unto me, how great shall be your joy with him in the kingdom of my Father!" (D&C 18:15).

Following the question and answer format: How great will be your joy? Suppose that you achieved exaltation with your spouse and now millions of years have passed away. You have created and peopled many earths like ours. You are standing together in your celestial kingdom surveying the creations you have made. The "cell phone" (i.e. celestial phone) rings and the voice on the other end greets you and asks if you have time for a quick visit. Since time is no longer a factor, you readily agree.

In an instant two beautiful, exalted beings are kneeling at your feet thanking you as only exalted beings can. You raise them up and then realize that it is a couple you taught and baptized while you were serving your mission. In fact they were the only baptisms you had. For years you had considered your mission a failure. Now, with them standing before you, tears coursing down their cheeks thanking you over and over again for the sacrifices you made in bringing the gospel to them, with a sweep of the hand, they open a vision of countless worlds they have created. You see the millions of their spirit children who are inhabiting and preparing to inhabit earths like ours. They turn to you and say: "All of these owe their existence to you! Without your sacrifice in bringing the gospel to us, we might never have gained our exaltation."

Now the joy you feel knows no bounds. Little did you know those many millions of years ago that endless worlds would attribute their existence and exaltation to you. Somehow I don't think our feeble, mortal minds can begin to comprehend what the Lord is promising when He explains the joy if our diligent labors bring many souls to Him. "And now, if your joy will be great with one soul that you have brought unto me into the kingdom of my Father, how great will be your joy if you should bring many souls unto me!" (D&C 18:16).

Will the sacrifices you make while serving, not only your full time mission but for the rest of your life, really be worth it? Depending on your trust in God and His word, you have your answer. You have no sure idea of what lies ahead of you. Some may be asked to lay down their lives in His service. Although that is a sobering thought, the Lord gives a comforting promise to those whose missions will result in physical death. "And whoso layeth down his life in my cause, for my name's sake, shall find it again, even life eternal.

"Therefore, be not afraid of your enemies, for I have decreed in my heart, saith the Lord, that I will prove you in all things, whether you will abide in my covenant, even unto death, that you may be found worthy" (D&C 98:13-14).

Very few, however, will be asked to make that magnitude of sacrifice. However, all of you will be asked to give up the comforts of home, jobs, and special friends, to postpone schooling and careers, to put God first in your lives. The promised blessings for doing so are not a few. You will profit from reading the scriptures and marking what the Savior says will come as a result of your willingness to sacrifice your wants to engage in His service. Here are three promised blessings:

> Therefore, O ye that embark in the service of God, see that ye serve him with all your heart, might, mind and strength, that ye may stand blameless before God at the last day.
>
> Therefore, if ye have desires to serve God ye are called to the work;
>
> For behold the field is white already to harvest; and lo, he that thrusteth in his sickle with his might, the same layeth up in store that he perisheth not, but bringeth salvation to his soul. (D&C 4:2-4)

First, if you'll serve with ALL of your heart, might, mind, and strength you will stand blameless before God at the day of judgment. Second, you will "perish not" or, in other words, you will not be burned at the Second Coming if you are still alive on the earth. If you have died before the Second Coming, the promise is that you will not fall short of your eternal potential. Third, you will bring salvation to your soul — you will gain the exaltation promised to the faithful. Not bad rewards for faithful service.

The Lord also said: "Therefore, thrust in your sickle with all your soul, and your sins are forgiven you, and you shall be laden with sheaves upon your back, for the laborer is worthy of his hire. Wherefore, your family shall live" (D&C 31:5). Here the Lord promises a forgiveness of sins if we do the work diligently. Additionally He promises "sheaves," or rewards for the hours and months of planting, weeding, watering and now harvesting. Sometimes the sheaves come in the form of convert baptisms, sometimes in other forms. Finally, this passage says that because of your labors ("wherefore" is like a scriptural "equals" sign), your family shall live. That may not always be realized in the short term. Sometimes terrible things happen to families of missionaries while they are serving. Put your trust in the Lord and eventually His promises shall all be fulfilled (see D&C 1:38).

Although the list could go on for many pages, one final reference will suffice. "Behold, I have seen your sacrifices, and will forgive all your sins; I have seen your sacrifices in obedience to that which I have told you. Go, therefore, and I make a way for your escape" (D&C 132:50). Which one of us would not like a clean slate to begin our post-mission life?

So here you stand at the brink of eternity. Prepared through countless years of pre-mortal schooling. Prepared to a limited degree by your efforts here in mortality. Excited beyond words because, after all these thousands of years, "the hour of your mission is come" (D&C 31:3). How should you view this once-in-a-lifetime mission? The Lord said: "Lift up your heart and rejoice" (D&C 31:3).

Don't worry about your family at home. The Lord said: "Verily, thus saith the Lord unto you, my friends, your families are well; they are in mine hands, and I will do with them as seemeth me good; for in me there is all power.
"Therefore, follow me, and listen to the counsel which I shall give unto you" (D&C 100:1-2).

Follow the counsel of your mission president and leaders, even if you don't fully understand or agree. The Lord will prosper you because of your obedience. Don't save up energy for some future battle. Now is the hour of your mission. You will not pass this way again as a young single missionary. How you serve during the next eighteen months or two years will chart the course for the rest of your life. So serve with honor and let the Lord honor you for the rest of your life and for eternity.

Who are you really? Perhaps Mormon's statement fits you best: "Behold, I am a disciple of Jesus Christ, the Son of God. I have been called of him to declare his word among his people, that they might have everlasting life" (3 Nephi 5:13). For the next year and a half or two years you are called to represent Him in declaring His gospel to a darkening world. President Harold B. Lee defines your title. He said, "The term 'elder,' which is applied to all holders of the Melchizedek Priesthood, means a **defender of the faith**. That is our prime responsibility and calling. Every holder of the Melchizedek Priesthood is to be a defender of the faith" (*Conference Report*, April 1970, p. 54).

Whether you are a sister missionary or an elder, you should be proud to be labeled as an **elder– a defender of the faith**. Let the Lord speak through you as you lose yourself in His service. No matter what perils you may be in, no matter what challenges await you, no matter how difficult the path or long the road, serve with honor. Be bold but not overbearing. Follow the Savior's invitation given to Enoch when he received his mission call. "Behold my Spirit is upon you, wherefore all thy words will I justify; and the mountains shall flee before you, and the rivers shall turn from their course; and thou shalt abide in me, and I in you; therefore **walk with me**" (Moses 6:34, emphasis added). There will likely be times when you'll think it would be easier to move mountains and divert rivers than to soften the hearts of some of your investigators. The Savior is just as willing to walk with you as He was with Enoch.

So, Elder or sister (defender of the faith), there is your challenge, your mission, and your opportunity for eternal greatness. Chosen thousands of years before you were born, now you have your chance to play on the Lord's first team in the final minutes of the fourth quarter of the super-bowl of all time. Play your heart out and win the prize.